♛ The
YUL BRYNNER
COOKBOOK

♛ The YUL BRYNNER COOKBOOK

Food Fit for the King and You

YUL BRYNNER
with Susan Reed

STEIN AND DAY/*Publishers*/New York

First published in 1983
Copyright © 1983 by Etc., Etc., Inc. and Susan Reed
All rights reserved Stein and Day, Incorporated
Designed by Louis A. Ditizio
Printed in the United States of America
STEIN AND DAY/*Publishers*
Scarborough House
Briarcliff Manor, N.Y. 10510

Library of Congress Cataloging in Publication Data

Brynner, Yul.
  The Yul Brynner cookbook.

  Includes index.
  1. Cookery, International.   I. Reed, Susan, 1946-
II. Title.
TX725.A1B79   1983   641.59   82-400005
ISBN 0-8128-2882-8

Contents

JAPANESE CUISINE

GYPSY CUISINE

SWISS CUISINE

CHINESE CUISINE

FRENCH CUISINE

THAI CUISINE

Introduction

Everyone knows that Yul Brynner is the King of Siam. Certainly when he takes the stage in the Rodgers & Hammerstein classic *The King and I*, it is clear that there never was and never will be a king quite like him.

Of course, Brynner is the kind of entertainer who tends to spoil an audience by consistently giving superb performances in all his chosen roles. In addition to the King of Siam, consider a few of his well-known film characters: Dimitri in *The Brothers Karamazov*, Chris the bandit leader of *The Magnificent Seven*, and Robot Gunslinger from *Westworld*. Brynner enriches all of these characters with a bigger-than-life quality. What's more, he does it so easily that instinct tells you the quality is an integral part of Brynner himself. His magnetic personality is so strong that you only have to see him to want to know more about him.

Here, obviously, is no ordinary individual. Yul Brynner has been a nightclub entertainer, a musician, a flyer from the high trapeze, a member of a traveling gypsy troupe, a professional jai alai player, and a director. He's currently one of the world's finest actors, the recipient of the Donaldson, Critics' Circle, Antoinette Perry (Tony), and Academy Awards. Besides his many professional achievements, he is an avid, expert photographer and holds a master's degree in science and philosophy from the Sorbonne in Paris. Additionally, Brynner is a loving father whose caring, active concern for all children endears him to countless youngsters. He's the author of *Bring Forth the Children,* a book written for the United Nations High Commission for Refugees. He enjoys traveling, and he possesses one of the greatest of all gifts: a natural facility with languages that easily allows him to be at home anywhere. (Brynner speaks eleven languages, including Russian, Chinese, Romany, Japanese, French, and English.) And where the average person would surely be content to have accomplished and experienced just a few of the many things Brynner has done and seen, Brynner himself continues to work tirelessly to finely tune his talents and to explore the joys of living. The man's energy is, quite simply, amazing.

How, one might reasonably ask, does he keep up his strength? Is it just a combination of personal will power and an insatiable drive to succeed that keeps him going or does he have a secret formula? Perhaps he guzzles copious amounts of liquid protein after his famous curtain calls. Or maybe he prizes hidden supplies of special exotic spices that he sprinkles onto his food. . . . Not really. There are no substitutes for talent, persistence and determination.

Yul Brynner *is* a gourmet, however, and since we are what we eat, knowing his favorite foods is really knowing about him. Here, then, are posed two simple questions: What does Yul Brynner eat? And what does he like best?

Like all of us, Brynner has definite preferences when it comes to food. His ancestry is Gypsy, Swiss, and Mongolian, which in part influences his culinary tastes. Gypsy cuisine is very hearty, robust, and inventive since so much of the cooking was developed by people who were constantly traveling, often from one country to another. The Swiss are especially famous for fondues, which Brynner enjoys immensely. Mongolian cooking is perhaps a bit too exotic, at least in execution, for the average household. Consider, for example, the Mongolian method of roasting lamb, which requires an entire unskinned animal. To prepare the lamb for roasting, remove the head and extract all the entrails through the neck opening. (The head, Yul says, is always prepared separately and served to the guest of honor.) Then dig a large pit and fill it with rocks the size of baseballs. Make a large fire on top of the rocks and when the fire has reduced itself to hot coals, mix the coals in with the rocks and wait until the rocks are heated through like charcoal. Next clean the inside of the lamb thoroughly and then fill the lamb cavity with the hot rocks. Sew the neck opening closed and set the lamb aside to roast—from the inside out! The most interesting thing to see in this entire process has to be the way the lamb cooks. Brynner notes that "First, the fur will all fall off the lamb, and the air will be filled with the marvelous aroma of the meat as it cooks. In a few hours, you can see that the outside is becoming cooked. The whole thing is ready to be eaten after three or four hours." Luckily for us, it is much easier to prepare gypsy and Swiss foods.

But what else influences Brynner's culinary tastes? Ah, here is a man who has tried everything, who has lived in Paris and Peking and New York, who has journeyed throughout Europe, America, and Asia. During his travels, Yul has sampled every conceivable (and sometimes inconceivable!) type of food—dishes prepared by professional chefs as well as dishes prepared by people who simply love to cook. His favorites range from classic recipes to easily prepared, quickly cooked goodies. And, of course, he has a few secret family recipes to share.

To give you an idea of the variety of Brynner's beloved foods, consider a colorful array of some of his chosen French specialties. Try a bit of the light and airy cheese soufflé, the pâté flavored with a hint of nutmeg. Sip the cream of carrot soup, which teases your taste buds with a touch of sherry, or the rich onion soup. Here's a watercress and endive salad, gently tossed with Yul's special favorite light salad dressing. Don't overlook the fresh mushrooms with cream, the ratatouille, or the pot roast provençale. Then sample the roulades de boeuf, or the blanquette de veau l'ancienne, some stuffed game hen with honey glaze, the bluefish normande cooked with dry cider, or the broiled salmon with smooth sour cream lemon sauce.

Perhaps you'd prefer sampling something from Asia, perhaps China. Consider Yul's special childhood favorite, chiao tze dumplings, which the family chef made for him as a special treat on Sundays only. Follow the dumplings with corn and crab soup, some of the tender ginger soy beef, lotus blossom spare ribs, refreshing asparagus salad, and New Year fried rice. And please pass the shredded soy chicken, the juicy simmered pork, the sweet and sour sea bass, and the Szechuan pepper beef.

Or maybe you'd like something Yul enjoyed when he was traveling with the gypsies? That would include hummus, pickled cucumbers, dandelion soup for the adventurous, and a fish soup almost thick enough to be a stew. There's also pork and sauerkraut ragout, chicken paprika with rich gravy and golden corn dumplings, a hearty beef goulash, red cabbage cooked with fresh apples, and a crisp-skinned portion of succulent roast goose.

No dessert? Don't be silly! How can you resist poppy-seed and honey cake, strawberries romanoff, green tea ice cream, almond fudge cake covered with freshly whipped cream and fresh raspberries, pears baked in wine with melted butter, or chunks of chiffon cake and fresh fruit waiting to be dipped into homemade chocolate fondue?

Of course, there's much more. From all of the food he enjoys, Brynner has selected Russian, Japanese, Gypsy, Swiss, Chinese, French, and Thai cuisines as being most meaningful to him. He personally associates each of these types of cooking with different stages of his life. Russian and Japanese foods are both part of the historical cuisine of Sakhalin Island, where Brynner was born. His mother was a gypsy, and his father was Swiss and Mongolian. Parts of Yul's childhood were spent in China and in France. Thailand? Well, Thailand was once known as Siam.

The Yul Brynner cookbook which you hold now is a veritable culinary biography. Whether you choose to mix and match dishes or to cook section by section, every time you use any recipe from this collection you'll be dining with Yul Brynner. The pleasures that are all his are about to become all yours as well. Follow the clear directions, and then sit right down and enjoy!

Susan Reed
New York City

♛ The YUL BRYNNER COOKBOOK

Cooking Tips and Hints

Cooking can be a rewarding creative endeavor that is a source of great pleasure and achievement. Whether you cook for yourself, your family, or friends, the time you take to provide nourishing delicious meals is also a way of showing that you care. And you don't need to spend all day in the kitchen to put together an impressive array of food. The recipes that follow include many one-dish meals that are prepared in the oven or in a dutch oven and require little work after all the ingredients are combined. Even when you choose a more complex menu, there are practical guidelines included in the directions that will help to ensure a successful outcome for everything you make. Please take the time to read through the following list of tips and hints. Above all remember that we want you to have fun cooking all of the dishes in this cookbook—and even more fun and pleasure enjoying the results.

1. Always read the recipe you select through from beginning to end before starting to cook. This way, you'll be familiar

with the steps for completing the dish and the cooking process itself will be smoother.

2. Pre-heat the oven first when so indicated in a recipe.

3. Assemble all necessary ingredients before you begin to cook. Use the best ingredients that you can obtain—the outcome of the recipe can be greatly affected by the quality of what goes into it. If a recipe calls for a fresh tomato, for instance, choose one that's vine-ripened since the flavor is usually richer than a hot house-ripened tomato.

4. Gather together all the appropriate utensils needed for each recipe before you start so that you don't have to hunt for a special knife or container after you've begun cooking.

5. Teaspoon and tablespoon measurements should be level, unless a recipe calls for a "heaping" amount which indicates a slightly larger quantity.

6. When using dried herbs such as basil or thyme that aren't powdered, crush the herbs between the palms of your hands to bring out their flavor.

7. When cooking with wines, it's acceptable to use a relatively inexpensive one. The alcohol will evaporate during the cooking process.

8. When using vegetables for making stocks, wash them but leave the skins intact. (Onions are the exception—peel them before adding to stock.)

9. Not all ovens provide constant and even heat; adjust the cooking time for each recipe according to the idiosyncrasies of your own oven.

10. When checking cakes and pastries to see if they're done, wait until the first half-hour of cooking has passed. Some cakes can fall if you open the oven too soon.

11. Don't be afraid to adjust spicing to your individual taste. Cooking is very much an art, and as such there's plenty of room for individual interpretation. Many of the recipes in this book use very little salt or pepper during the cooking process, for example, and indicate instead their addition according to taste after the dish is cooked.

About Substitutions

Commercial broths may be substituted for soup and gravy stocks. Substitutions can also be made for some of the spices in the Japanese, Chinese, and Thai sections; they're indicated in each section. We do encourage you to investigate ordering by mail from the stores listed at the end of this book, however, when you can't obtain everything you need locally. The authentic flavors of more exotic foods are well worth the extra effort. Any spices or ingredients that you order can be stored and used as you continue to explore cooking new dishes. If you make a stock that is not as rich as you like, try adding an appropriately flavored bouillon cube to enhance the flavor.

Russian Cuisine

Introduction

My birthplace, Sakhalin Island, is a small, narrow bit of land north of Japan and just off the southeastern coast of Russia. Two parallel mountain ranges run partway down Sakhalin's 560 mile length; the width of the island varies from 17 to 140 miles. The climate is subarctic, the mean temperature just barely freezing. The local people earn their livings by fishing, mining, and some limited farming. Until the mid-1940s, Sakhalin was alternately claimed by Russia and Japan. At one time, in the mid-1800s, the two countries shared control of the island. Now, the population is mostly Russian, and Sakhalin, along with the Kuril Islands, forms a Russian province.

I was only six months old when I left Sakhalin. My father, anxious to return home to China where the family business was then centered, waited only until I was strong enough to survive the journey before starting out. On the way to China we stopped in Vladivostok, at Russia's extreme southeastern tip, to register my birth. Sakhalin was intensely rural, and Vladivostok was the very first

7

town we came to that was big enough to have a public official who could record the birth. Although I did not grow up in Russia or on Sakhalin I have a deep love for the Slavic food served there.

Russia's culinary heritage is truly magnificent. In the czars' time, Russian nobility entertained in grand style, serving guests food set out on tableware often made of gilded silver, gold, and enamel. A continuous parade of food was marched before admiring eyes four times a day. In addition to breakfast, lunch, and dinner, it was the custom to serve predinner appetizers called zakuski. It was hard to tell the difference between zakuski and dinner, such was the quantity and quality of those appetizers. They were set out on a separate table, and included such delicacies as caviar, individual stuffed meat and vegetable pies, assorted pickled fish, plain and pickled vegetables, various pâtés, smoked fish, and smoked eel. With the announcement of dinner came an assortment of soups such as borsch and cabbage soup; larger pies stuffed with chopped egg, meat, and mushrooms or sauerkraut; game birds such as grouse and partridge; roast meats and fish.

After the main courses were cleared away it was time for dessert, for those who wisely had saved some room. Rich cakes and thickened fruit purees were favorites. Those who weren't of noble blood dined more simply, and, some might say, much more sensibly, on soup, kasha, vegetables, cheese and basic meat or poultry dishes. Whatever the social level of the host, any guest in a Russian home would be served ample and generous portions. Today Slavic hospitality still requires that every plate be filled to overflowing; it's a tradition established to make you feel welcome and very much at home.

Winters in most of Russia are very long and bitterly cold, and today's Slavic cuisine, while occasionally somewhat less exotic than in czarist times, is robust and hearty, designed to give sustenance to the spirit as well as to the body. Certainly foods such as rich soups garnished with sour cream, a thick slice of black bread spread heavily with fresh butter, stuffed cabbage, beef Stroganoff, and chicken pilaf help dispel the effects of cold weather.

Foods serve the opposite purpose, too, and the often stifling heat of summer can be eased with a big bowl of chilled borsch, avocado stuffed with sour cream and caviar, salad made with meat and potatoes, and some strawberries Romanoff.

One of the Russian specialties I enjoy year-round is blini. Blini are thin golden-brown pancakes made with buckwheat flour; they are cooked in melted butter and garnished with sour cream and caviar. I've heard that when you eat these particular pancakes, you're actually helping to preserve an ancient custom. In the old days, blini were made early each spring. The pancakes represented the sun, and that strengthening spring sun foretold another season of growth and continued life. People believed that by eating blini they shared in the sun's power; they also showed their awe of and respect for the sun. In this dish, symbolism is also evident in the caviar garnish. A delicacy reputed to impart longevity, caviar in Russia displays a host's wealth and highlights a guest's importance.

In its entirety, the Union of Soviet Socialist Republics encompasses every climate from the extreme cold of the arctic north to the subtropical south. Much of the land is essentially flat, a seemingly endless plain only occasionally interrupted by mountainous regions. Land that cannot be used for agriculture—the tundra, marshes, and desert—is counter-balanced by the Baltic states' fertile farm land and the rich, black soil of the Ukrainian steppes. While fish, meat, poultry, and grains are usually available in adequate supply, fresh fruits and vegetables are abundant only during the short growing seasons. Preserves and pickled or canned vegetables help provide variety in the Russian diet. And in the streets of large cities such as Moscow and Leningrad, vendors sell sausage, black bread, ice cream made from fresh cream, sugar and eggs, and kvass, an extremely low-alcohol beverage made from fermented black bread.

As you enjoy the recipes that follow, consider serving vodka along with many of them. To drink vodka in the authentic Russian manner, pour it into small glasses and swallow it all at once instead of sipping it. Zakuski are usually served with vodka, especially since enthusiasts are known to alternate bites of food with glasses of vodka, a habit which requires a great deal of intestinal fortitude. Although most vodka served outside the Soviet Union is clear and unflavored, Russians often use lemon peel, berries, or even peppercorns to give their vodka a little extra taste. You may also serve other beverages such as carbonated fruit juices and tea. The Russian version of soda pop is much less sweet than that served here in the West because the Soviets add much less syrup and sometimes make fruit drinks by simply adding crushed fruit to slightly sweetened water. Tea in the U.S.S.R. is brewed to maximum strength in a small pot and then individual cups of the brew are diluted to taste with boiling water from a samovar.

Whatever you decide goes best with your meal, I'm sure your guests will want second helpings.

Avocado with Caviar

The combination of sour cream and caviar (fish roe, fish eggs) will give almost any dish a Russian flavor. Caviar is used in this recipe as a garnish, and it really livens up the mild avocado. When choosing caviar, keep in mind that the finest and most popular fish roe comes from the sturgeon. Beluga, the largest sturgeon, also produces the largest, choicest eggs, which are dark gray or black. Fine caviar is prepared by hand; the membranes surrounding the fish eggs are removed and a touch of salt is added. Less choice caviar is always more heavily salted. ("Less choice," with reference to caviar, doesn't mean that the caviar isn't perfectly acceptable. Like all foods, it's a matter of taste.) Purists use only silver spoons to serve and eat caviar, claiming that other metals leave an aftertaste.

This dish is very good during hot summer months, and can be served as an appetizer or as a main course year round.

2 ripe avocados	1 hard-cooked egg, chopped
½ fresh lemon	1 small raw onion, minced
1 cup sour cream	2 cups shredded lettuce
4 teaspoons caviar	

Cut ripe avocados in half lengthwise; remove pit. Sprinkle flesh with fresh lemon juice to prevent discoloration. Fill each cavity with ¼ cup sour cream. Top sour cream with 1 teaspoon caviar, and then sprinkle with chopped egg and minced onion. Serve in individual bowls on a bed of shredded lettuce. *(Serves 4)*

Russian Meat Salad

Russian salads are hearty and easily can be enjoyed as main dishes. They almost always combine a variety of meats and vegetables with a full-flavored dressing. To round out the salad if you're serving it as a meal, garnish with fresh tomatoes, scallions, and radishes.

1 cup cooked cubed beef	2 tablespoons wine vinegar
1 cup cooked cubed chicken	½ teaspoon fresh lemon juice
1 cup cooked diced potatoes	½ teaspoon mustard
½ cup cooked green peas	Salt, pepper
1 cooked carrot, sliced	2 chopped hard-cooked eggs
¼ cup chopped dill pickle	1 tablespoon capers
¼ cup olive oil	Dill

Combine beef, chicken, potatoes, peas, carrot, and pickle in a large bowl. Mix together oil, vinegar, lemon juice, and mustard. Add salt and pepper to taste. Pour dressing over salad and mix well. Add chopped egg and capers; stir again, sprinkle with dill, and serve on crisp lettuce. *(Serves 4)*

Marinated Mushrooms

This is one of the dishes that was a staple on the zakuski table. Serve it as an appetizer, a side dish, or a salad on a bed of lettuce. The mushrooms can be stored in the refrigerator for quite some time, if you have any left over.

1 pound fresh mushrooms	¼ teaspoon dry mustard
¾ cup vegetable oil	Dash salt
¼ cup red wine vinegar	4–6 black peppercorns
1 bay leaf	Pinch of dill

Use small, white mushrooms of uniform size. Wash mushrooms and set aside to drain. Combine oil, vinegar, bay leaf, mustard, salt, and peppercorns in a saucepan. Bring to boil, reduce heat, and simmer marinade for several minutes. Add drained mushrooms, stir, and simmer for 2–3 minutes. Remove mushrooms from heat, cool, and place them in a glass bowl or wide mouth jar. Sprinkle pinch of dill over mushrooms, stir, and refrigerate for 24 hours before serving. *(Serves 4 as appetizer)*

Stuffed Cabbage

When stuffing cabbage leaves, begin by placing the filling about two fingers' width from the thinnest edge of the leaf (top edge). Then cover the filling with that exposed top edge of the leaf, and fold in the sides of the leaf to prevent the filling from escaping. Continue rolling the leaf from the top edge to the bottom, thick part. Trim off any excess part of the thick end of the cabbage leaf, once the roll is completed.

1 medium white cabbage	2 tablespoons tomato puree
2 tablespoons butter	3 tablespoons raisins
1 medium onion, chopped fine	3 tablespoons vinegar or lemon
1 clove garlic	juice
1 pound ground beef	3 tablespoons sugar
1 teaspoon dill	1 cup cooked white rice
½ teaspoon salt	3 tablespoons butter
¼ teaspoon black pepper	1 cup sour cream (optional)
2 cups chicken stock	

Fill a large soup pot with water, and place over high heat until water boils. While water is heating, remove outer leaves from cabbage, and cut out the cabbage core. Discard outer leaves and core. Separate the remaining cabbage leaves, taking care not to tear them, and cook them for about ten minutes in the boiling water. If the leaves do not separate easily, put the entire head of cabbage into the boiling water. Peel the leaves away carefully as the cabbage cooks. The leaves should be medium-soft and translucent in appearance when you take them out of the water. Set the leaves aside to cool.

In a large skillet, melt 2 tablespoons butter, and saute the chopped onion and garlic clove in the melted butter. Remove the garlic clove, and add 1 pound ground beef, dill, salt, and pepper. Brown the meat thoroughly, and, when it's cooked, drain off excess fat and remove cooked beef from the heat. Combine stock, tomato puree, raisins, vinegar or lemon juice, and sugar in a sauce pan. Bring to boil and then reduce heat so that sauce simmers. Mix the cooked rice with the cooked beef. Preheat oven to 350° F.

Stuff individual cabbage leaves with 2–3 tablespoons of rice and meat filling to form cabbage rolls. (Rolls should look like oblong cylinders.) Place cabbage rolls in a single layer in a large, shallow baking dish. Pour hot sauce over the cabbage, and bake covered for 30 minutes. After 30 minutes, turn cabbage rolls, re-cover dish, and bake another 20 minutes. After 20 minutes, turn rolls once more, dot with 3 tablespoons butter, and bake uncovered for the last 10 minutes. Serve with sour cream to garnish, if desired. *(Serves 4)*

Blini

The pancakes this recipe yields are light and fluffy for two reasons. First, the batter contains yeast and is allowed to rise. Second, stiffly beaten egg whites are folded into the batter. The resulting blini are guaranteed to melt in your mouth.

2 cups milk	3 egg yolks
¼ cup very warm water	3 tablespoons sour cream
1 teaspoon sugar	1 teaspoon sugar
1 package dry yeast	3 tablespoons melted butter
1½ cup white flour	3 egg whites
1 cup buckwheat flour	1 tablespoon butter per
½ teaspoon salt	pancake for cooking

Heat milk in a saucepan until it just reaches the boiling point. Remove from heat and set aside to cool. When milk has cooled, remove the thin "skin" that has formed on top. In a small bowl, combine warm water, sugar, and yeast. Sift flours and salt together into another bowl. In a large mixing bowl, combine yeast mixture with 1 cup scalded, cooled milk. Add 1 cup flour mixture, mixing until just well-blended. Cover the bowl with a large plate or pot cover, and let stand for 30 minutes.

Beat the egg yolks slightly, and combine them with the sour cream, sugar, and melted butter. Add this mixture and the remaining milk and flour to the large bowl. Blend well, cover again, and let rise until doubled in volume. At this point, beat egg whites until stiff. *Fold* whites into batter, and let stand covered 15 minutes.

To cook blini, melt 1 tablespoon of butter in a 7″ skillet for each pancake. Add enough batter to the pan to almost cover the bottom, and cook on the first side until bubbles form on the surface and the bottom of the pancake is lightly browned. Turn and cook on the second side. Keep cooked blini warm in a very low oven while you continue making the pancakes until the batter is all used. *(Serves 4)*

Blini Garnish

The best, most traditional way to serve blini is to spread each pancake with a generous amount of sour cream and caviar to taste. Top these garnishes with melted butter and then roll up the blini like jelly rolls. Serve immediately.

Chilled Fruit Soup

Fruit soup is the perfect dish to serve in the hot weather when you want something just a little bit different. It even can be served as a dessert.

4 large ripe peaches	½ cup dry white wine
8 large ripe plums	⅛ teaspoon cardamom
2 cups ripe cherries	Dash of cinnamon
¾ cup water	Sour cream
½ cup sugar (more or less to taste)	

Peel and slice peaches, discarding pits. Slice plums, leaving the skin on the fruit and discarding the pits. Remove pits from cherries, and place all fruit into a medium-size saucepan. Add water and sugar, then bring fruit mixture to boil. Reduce heat, and simmer gently until fruit is soft. Add wine and spices (also add more sugar if you wish), and bring to a boil for several minutes, stirring frequently. Remove mixture from the heat, and then cool it. Puree in a blender or food processor, and chill. Serve well-chilled and garnished with sour cream to taste. *(Serves 6)*

Beef Stock

The three soups below are all made with beef stock. You can use commercial beef stock or broth if you wish, or make your own stock following this recipe.

1 pound lean brisket of beef
Several large cracked beef
   marrow bones
1 large onion, peeled
2 carrots, sliced in several
   pieces

2 celery stalks, tops included,
   sliced in several pieces
3 bay leaves
8 black peppercorns
10 cups water

Put all of the above into large soup pot. Bring to a boil, reduce heat, and simmer for at least 3 hours. Skim off any residue that rises to the top of the stock. After 3 hours, remove and discard beef bones and vegetables. Set the brisket aside, cool the stock slightly, and then strain it. Pour the stock into a large soup pot.

Cabbage Soup

4 tablespoons butter
1 cup sliced onions, cut into
   quarters after slicing
2 cups shredded white cabbage
2 sliced ripe tomatoes, cut into
   halves after slicing
¼ cup red wine vinegar

½ teaspoon salt
2 tablespoons sugar
¼ teaspoon black pepper
Brisket from the stock
Sour cream
6 hot, boiled white potatoes
   (optional)

Melt butter in a large skillet. Sauté onions and cabbage in butter until fairly soft. Add tomatoes, vinegar, salt, sugar, and pepper to the skillet. Stir to blend, and add vegetables to the soup pot with the beef stock. Bring soup to boiling point, reduce heat, and simmer slowly for 30 minutes. Cut the brisket into small pieces; add the pieces of meat to the soup, and heat through. Serve garnished with sour cream, and, if desired, add a boiled potato to each bowl of soup. *(Serves 6)*

Borsch

There are two basic types of borsch (borscht). One is a simple beet soup, served hot or cold. The other is a hearty meat and vegetable soup. Since they are equally delicious, recipes for both follow.

Simple Borsch

8 cups beef stock (see recipe)
2 tablespoons butter
1 medium onion
4 large beets
½ cup red wine vinegar (more, if you like a very tart taste)

3 tablespoons sugar
1 cup sour cream
Salt
Pepper

Bring the beef stock to boiling point in a large soup pot. Reduce heat so that stock simmers. Melt butter in a medium-sized skillet. Peel onion and chop into small pieces. Sauté onion in butter, and, while the onion is cooking, remove the skin from the beets and cut beets into strips by first slicing each beet and then cutting the slices into strips no wider than ¼ inch. (You should have about 4 cups of beets.) Add the cooked onions and beet strips to the stock. Cover and simmer for one hour, then add vinegar and sugar so that you have a sweet/sour blend. Cover and simmer 30 minutes. Just before serving, stir in 1 cup soup cream. Season to taste with salt and pepper. *(Serves 6-8)*

Garnish for Cold Borsch

If you serve borsch cold, sprinkle the top with fresh dill, and add cucumber slices that have been peeled and from which the seeds are removed. This is a wonderful soup to serve in hot weather.

Hearty Borsch

8 cups beef stock	⅓ cup red wine vinegar
4 tablespoons butter	1–2 tablespoons sugar
1 large onion	2 bay leaves
4 large beets	½ pound cooked ham
2 tomatoes	Brisket from soup stock
2 carrots	Salt, pepper
1 celery stalk	1 cup sour cream
1 small turnip	

Bring stock to boiling point in a large soup pot. Reduce heat, and let stock simmer. Melt butter in a medium-size skillet. Peel onion and chop into small pieces. Sauté onion, and cut peeled beets into strips as directed for Simple Borsch. Chop tomatoes into large pieces. Peel and slice carrots into thin slices. Dice celery stalk. Peel turnip, and dice into small pieces. Add all vegetables to the simmering stock. Continue simmering for one hour, or until all vegetables are tender. Add vinegar, sugar, and bay leaves to soup. Simmer 30 minutes. Dice ham and brisket, and add the meats to the soup. Season with salt and pepper, and garnish with sour cream. *(Serves 6–8)*

Ukrainian Pyrogy (called Pyrohïh)

I love the small pastry dough pies that the Russians fill with a wide variety of different combinations of meat and vegetables. I've sampled pirojhki, as the pies are called, which have been deepfried or baked after being stuffed with chopped meat, hard-boiled egg, rice with onion and butter, mushrooms and cream, or even sauerkraut, a food that was brought to Russia by Mongol warriors. I've also enjoyed the dish which was popular before the individual pies and from which they derive; it is a very large rectangular pastry called a pirog, which can be filled with equal parts of chopped beef, chicken, veal, onions, and mushrooms, and lots of butter to ward off the chill of Russian winters. A pirog is baked and then cut into individual servings. An interesting variation is the Ukrainian pyrohih (pih-row-hih), which are first boiled and then lightly heated with fried onion bits and melted butter. These pies are filled with cooked mashed potato and cottage cheese and are wonderful with a generous serving of sour cream.

There are several steps in making pyrohih. First you make the dough, which you roll out and cut into 3" diameter circles. Next you make the filling, which you place inside each dough circle and enclose to make a crescent. Crimp the open edges shut. The pyrohih are then boiled and put aside while you cook onion in butter and then heat the pyrohih in the same cooking pan. Serve these cooked pies as appetizers or as your main course.

Dough:

2 cups flour	½ cup water
2 eggs	½ teaspoon salt

Combine the above ingredients and mix to form a stiff dough. Divide the dough into two equal parts. Set one dough ball aside, and roll the other one out on a floured board to no more than ⅛" thickness. Using a round cookie cutter with a 3-inch diameter, cut out circles of dough. Combine dough scraps together, and continue to roll out dough until as many circles as possible are cut out. Do the same with the second dough ball. *(Makes 24 circles, and should be enough to serve 4)*

Filling:

1 cup cottage cheese (not too moist—drain off any excess liquid)	1 cup mashed potatoes Salt, pepper

Combine all the above filling ingredients in a medium-size bowl. Place 1-2 teaspoons of filling in the center of each dough circle. Fold circles in half, and pinch edges together to make a crescent. Moisten edges slightly if the dough does not seal easily. (Any extra filling may be shaped into small patties and fried.)

To cook:

Fill a large kettle with water. Add a small amount of salt, and bring water to a boil. Place individual pyrohih on a large, slotted spoon, and place a few pyrohih at a time into the boiling water. After a few moments they'll rise to the top of the water. Continue cooking another 8-10 minutes, remove from water, and drain. Cook remaining pyrohih in the same manner. When all the pies are cooked, prepare the following:

1 large onion, peeled and
   chopped

8 tablespoons butter

After chopping the onion, melt the butter in a large skillet. Add onion pieces, and sauté slowly until onions are transparent. Then add pyrohih to the skillet and gently heat them, turning each pie so that it becomes coated with butter and cooked onions. The pyrohih shouldn't fry; you just want to heat them and coat them with the butter and onion. As soon as this is done, put the pyrohih into a large serving bowl or onto a large platter. Pour any butter and onion remaining in the skillet over the pyrohih. Serve with the following:

Garnish:

Sour cream

Chopped fresh parsley

Potatoes Baked
with Sour Cream

6–8 cups boiling, salted water
  3 cups peeled, sliced white
     potatoes
  4 tablespoons butter
  1 medium onion
  1 cup sour cream
  1 egg, beaten
  ½ teaspoon dill

  ½ teaspoon caraway seeds
  ½ teaspoon salt
  ¼ teaspoon black pepper
  ½ cup bread crumbs
  ⅛ cup parmesan cheese
     (optional)
  2 tablespoons butter

Bring 6–8 cups of water to boil in a saucepan. Add small amount of salt to the water. Add potatoes to the boiling water, and cook for 10 minutes, or until potatoes are softened but not cooked through. Drain water off potatoes and set aside. Preheat oven to 350° F. Melt butter in a skillet. Peel and chop onion; sauté in butter. Put sour cream into a bowl; add cooked onion, butter, and beaten egg; stir. Add dill, caraway seeds, salt, and pepper to the sour cream mixture; stir again.

Lightly butter a casserole dish. Layer potatoes and the sour cream mixture, ending with sour cream. Sprinkle bread crumbs over the sour cream, and, if desired, sprinkle cheese on top of the crumbs. Dot with butter, and bake 35–40 minutes, or until a knife inserted in the dish goes through all the layers easily. *(Serves 4)*

Marinated Lamb

This marinade can be used for lamb roasts, shish kebob, or, my favorite, lamb chops. Hard cider is preferable, but you can use regular apple cider if you wish.

Marinade:

1 cup hard apple cider
½ cup red wine vinegar
1 medium onion
1 clove garlic
¼ cup water

1 bay leaf
1 tablespoon sugar
¼ teaspoon freshly chopped
   ginger

2 pounds lamb chops

Combine cider and vinegar. Peel the onion and cut it into 8 pieces. Put the onion and all the remaining ingredients with the cider and vinegar. Mix well and pour over lamb. Marinate overnight, and then broil meat to taste. Baste with marinade during cooking. *(Serves 4)*

Beef Stroganoff

If you've made beef stock, save a cup of it for this classic dish, which I like served over hot buttered noodles sprinkled with poppy seeds.

2 pounds beef tenderloin	2 teaspoons Worcestershire
2 tablespoons flour	sauce
6 tablespoons butter	2 cups sliced mushrooms (fresh
1 large onion, minced	preferred)
1 cup beef stock	1 cup sour cream
½ cup dry red wine	Salt and pepper

Cut beef into strips about ¼″ wide by ½″ thick by several inches long. Sprinkle flour evenly over beef. Melt butter in a large skillet. Sauté minced onion in butter. Add meat, cooking on all sides until well browned. Add stock, wine, and Worcestershire sauce to meat. Bring to boil, reduce heat, cover, and simmer for one hour or until meat is very tender. Then add mushrooms, and cook for 3–4 minutes. Add sour cream, and stir to blend with the sauce in the pan. Heat until cream is heated just through. Season to taste with salt and pepper, and serve at once. *(Serves 4)*

Chicken Kiev

This is a marvelous dish to serve for special occasions. It's really simple to prepare, and watching your guests' surprise and delight at finding melted butter inside crispy chicken is well worth the extra care necessary for Chicken Kiev. If you follow each step exactly, the butter will stay inside the chicken until it's served.

2 eggs
1 tablespoon water
¾ cup flour
1½ cup bread crumbs
1 tablespoon parsley (fresh
    if possible—or use ½
    tablespoon dried parsley)
1 teaspoon thyme
½ teaspoon salt

¼ teaspoon black pepper
8 chicken breasts, bones
    removed
16 tablespoons chilled sweet
    butter
Vegetable oil in deep fryer

Cooked rice (optional—see
    note)

Beat eggs slightly with water in a large, shallow dish. Combine flour, bread crumbs, herbs, and spices in a separate large, shallow dish. Prepare chicken as follows:

Cut off the small, narrow piece of chicken attached to the breast. Place the small piece of meat and the breast between two pieces of wax paper. Pound the meat with a mallet until it's about ⅛" thick. (The edges of the larger piece of chicken should be extra thin. This makes it easier to seal the meat around the butter filling in the next step.) Make a cylinder of 2 tablespoons of chilled sweet butter. Place the butter in the center of the breast meat. Cover the butter with the small piece of chicken. Fold one of the long ends of the chicken breast up over the butter, fold in the two short ends, and bring over the other long end. Press down the edges to seal. Repeat procedure for each chicken filet.

Dip each wrapped chicken cutlet in the egg mixture, and then coat well with the flour/bread crumb/herb/spice mixture. Place the coated chicken on a platter, and chill in the refrigerator for at least one hour. (This is a very important step; it helps keep the butter inside the chicken as it cooks.)

When ready to cook the chicken, first preheat vegetable oil in a deep fryer to 360° F. (A deep skillet with oil several inches deep and a frying basket may also be used.) Fry as many cutlets as possible at a time without layering pieces. Fry until golden brown—at least five minutes. If chicken is cooked in more than one batch, cooked pieces can be kept warm in a slightly heated oven. Serve immediately as soon as all the chicken is cooked. *(Serves 4)*

Note: I like putting the chicken on a bed of rice. If any butter escapes, it goes onto the rice and is delicious.

I like the typical Russian accompaniment of green peas with the chicken and rice. For variety, try kasha or potatoes instead of rice.

Chicken Pilaf

This quick dish is a great way to use leftovers from a roast chicken or roast turkey.

2 tablespoons butter	2 medium tomatoes, chopped
1 medium onion, peeled and chopped	1 bay leaf
	2 cups chicken broth
1 clove garlic	½ cup sliced mushrooms (fresh,
1 cup uncooked rice	if possible)
2 cups cooked chicken cut in small pieces	Salt and pepper

Melt butter in a large skillet. Sauté chopped onion and garlic clove until onions are transparent. Remove garlic clove. Add uncooked rice and sauté until rice is also transparent. Add chicken pieces, chopped tomatoes, bay leaf, and chicken broth. Stir once, cover skillet, and reduce heat so that broth simmers. Cook until the rice is almost done—approximately 15 minutes. Add mushrooms, cover, and continue cooking until rice is soft. Season to taste with salt and pepper, and serve. *(Serves 4)*

Steamed Stuffed Trout

The stuffing for this fish contains raisins and almonds and is almost a meal in itself. In combination with the trout, it's heavenly. (Please try to make this with fresh trout; it makes a considerable difference. I prefer all fish recipes to be made with fresh fish.)

4 fresh trout with backbone removed	¼ cup chicken broth
6 tablespoons sweet butter	1 egg, well beaten
1 small onion, chopped	1¼ cup dry white wine
½ cup white raisins	¼ cup chicken broth
½ cup slivered almonds	1 tablespoon dry sherry
1 cup bread crumbs	¼ teaspoon salt
⅛ teaspoon salt	1 tablespoon fresh lemon juice
Pinch of white pepper	1 cup sour cream
1 tablespoon fresh parsley, chopped	4 tablespoons melted sweet butter
	1 fresh lemon, thinly sliced

(Ask that the backbone be removed when you purchase the fish. Have fish steamer handy—or see note.) Wash trout, removing any remaining bones which may be left. Dry fish well, and set aside. Melt butter in a medium-size skillet. Sauté chopped onion. Add raisins and nuts to the skillet. Lower heat, and allow raisins to heat through. Meanwhile, combine bread crumbs, salt, pepper, and parsley in a large bowl. Add onions, nuts, raisins, and melted butter to the bowl. Mix well, and then moisten with chicken broth and beaten egg. Mix well again, and divide into four equal amounts. Stuff fish with dressing and set aside.

Remove tray from fish steamer, and lightly coat top of tray with butter. Arrange fish on the steamer tray, and put the tray into the fish steamer. Combine wine, chicken broth, sherry, salt, and lemon juice. Pour around fish in steamer, cover, and steam for 10–12 minutes, or until the fish gently flakes when tested with a fork. Arrange cooked trout on a serving platter. Cover each fish with equal amounts of sour cream and melted sweet butter. Arrange lemon slices around the fish, and serve. *(Serves 4)*

Note: The fish may also be steamed in the oven. Preheat the oven to 325° F. Place fish on a buttered baking rack that fits inside a larger baking dish. Add wine mixture to bottom of the baking dish, cover dish, and cook fish for 25–30 minutes, or until it flakes when tested with a fork.

Apple Walnut Cake

This is one of my favorite cakes; it's so rich, it doesn't need any icing, just a sprinkling of confectioner's sugar. I recommend that you use a food processor or blender to chop the apples and walnuts.

3 cups peeled chopped apples	½ teaspoon salt
1 cup butter	1 teaspoon cinnamon
2 cups sugar	½ teaspoon nutmeg
3 eggs	¼ teaspoon allspice
¼ cup sour cream	3 teaspoons vanilla
3 cups flour	1 cup chopped walnuts
1½ teaspoons baking soda	Confectioner's sugar

Preheat oven to 325° F. Butter and flour a tube pan; set aside. Peel and remove core from several large cooking apples. Chop the apples, preferably in food processor or blender, and set aside. (Pieces should be approximately the size of one-half a plump raisin—certainly no larger.) Cream the butter and sugar together in a large bowl. Add eggs and mix well. Add sour cream, blend, and set aside. Sift together flour, baking soda, and spices. Gradually add flour mixture to sour cream mixture. Add vanilla, blend well.

Stir apples and walnuts into batter, which will be very thick. Pour batter into tube pan, and bake as directed above for about one hour. Test cake after 55 minutes by inserting a toothpick into the center of the cake. If toothpick comes out clean, cake is done. Remove cake from oven when done, cool 15 minutes, and remove from pan. When cake is thoroughly cooled, sprinkle lightly with confectioner's sugar. *(Serves 8-10)*

Kisel

Kisel is a thickened fruit purée. I think of it as an elegant fruit pudding, the perfect dessert to serve after a large meal. This recipe calls for raspberries, but you can substitute other fruits according to individual taste.

2 cups fresh raspberries
1½ cups water
⅔ cup sugar (or to taste)
¼ cup cornstarch or potato
   starch

½ cup water

1 cup heavy cream, whipped if
   desired

Cook raspberries in water until the berries are very soft—about five minutes. Remove berries from heat, and purée in blender or food processor. Return puréed fruit to cooking pot, add sugar, stir, and cook over low heat. Combine cornstarch or potato starch and ½ cup water. Gradually add to fruit, stirring constantly until mixture thickens. (Note: For a thinner kisel, add only part of starch/water mixture. It thickens as it cooks. Judge according to preference.) Remove from heat, pour into bowl, and chill. Garnish with heavy cream, plain or whipped, just before serving. *(Serves 4)*

Strawberries Romanoff

My favorite way of preparing this dessert is to use homemade ice cream, but many commercial brands are perfectly fine substitutes.

1 pint vanilla ice cream	1 cup heavy cream
2 cups fresh strawberries	2 tablespoons sugar
1–2 tablespoons kirsch	¼ teaspoon vanilla extract
2 tablespoons sugar	¼ cup sour cream

Set ice cream aside at room temperature to soften. Wash berries, remove stems, slice, and sprinkle with kirsch and sugar in a small bowl. Set aside. In another bowl, whip the heavy cream, gradually adding 2 tablespoons of sugar to the cream as it thickens. Add vanilla, and set aside. Put softened ice cream into a large bowl. Stir sour cream into ice cream. Fold whipped cream into mixture, put mixture into large ice cube tray, and refreeze. When ready to serve, layer frozen cream mixture and strawberries in parfait glasses. *(Serves 4)*

Japanese Cuisine

==

Introduction

I love seafood, particularly the seafood of the Japanese Islands, where virtually no food is overcooked or overseasoned, and where many fish dishes are traditionally served uncooked. On my last visit to Japan, I strolled through the fish market and chose a meal of freshly caught small gray shrimp and whitebait. The shrimp, not available anywhere else, are so tender that you can just pop them into your mouth and eat them without removing their shells. My two small daughters, Mia and Melody, enjoy them for snacks and they swear that the shrimp taste just like fresh cherries. Whitebait is a more exotic food. They're very small young fish, so tiny that fishermen must use gauzelike nets to capture them. These fish are presented swimming in a small cup and are eaten while they're still alive.

Granted, eating whitebait is not for everyone, and it's undeniably an extreme concept for the uninitiated. But, considered simply, whitebait is nothing more than a pure example of freshness. As such it's a great delicacy in Japan, where great emphasis is placed on maintaining a food's natural flavor. Sushi and sashimi, two other popular uncooked fish dishes, pass the flavor test equally well. Eating nigiri sushi, which are small pieces of tender fish and shrimp served on individual mounds of slightly vinegared rice seasoned with Japanese horseradish, is an ideal way to sample the excellence of uncooked fish, particularly if you're doing so for the first time. When you take a bite of sushi, you'll discover that uncooked fish has a delicate, very mild flavor and a pleasing texture. As your taste for sushi develops, you'll soon graduate to sashimi, small slices of fish filets eaten without rice. Both sushi and sashimi, by the way, are high in protein and low in calories. They're served with shoyu (Japanese soy sauce) and gari (pickled ginger slices) as accompaniments.

Meat and poultry are certainly available and are served often in Japan. Yakitori (marinated and skewered chicken) and shabu-shabu, a meat and vegetable dish cooked right at the table, are old standbys. Some recipes, like teriyaki, work equally well with fish, poultry, or meat. Seafood, however, is the favorite food of that country, which is surrounded by rich fishing waters. The abundance and variety of fish is astounding; each seasonal change brings a different selection to the market. And yes, fish is also served cooked. It's baked, broiled, steamed, or coated with a batter and quickly deep-fried. Actually, fish in one form or another is served at almost every meal.

The Japanese are a singularly courteous people, and no experience is more civilized than a Japanese dinner. Dining etiquette requires that hunger never be displayed. Good manners require that one demonstrate a sense of well-being and relaxation at the table. To help achieve the correct mood, even the dining environment exudes peace and tranquility. In a typical Japanese dining area, for example, one thoughtfully chosen spray of flowers and perhaps a single wall hanging may convey serenity. If you concentrate on the subtle and muted colors of the wall hanging, you may suddenly notice that the flowers have been freshly picked and are placed in exactly the right position so that the light in the room is gently reflected off the moisture on the flower petals. The colors are all coordinated to induce a feeling of calm; taking just a few minutes to appreciate them can help you forget any worries.

For a formal meal, everyone sits before a low table on soft cushions which are placed directly on mats covering the floor. Shoes are not worn in the dining area since soles are dirty. Instead, guests wear soft, clean slippers. All of these things further contribute to a clear mind and a relaxed body. The Japanese firmly believe that only when this state of harmony is reached can a person enjoy food completely. Now, and only now, are you fully ready to appreciate the pleasures of eating and replenishing the body. Before anything is served, however, small, tightly rolled hand towels moistened with very hot, lightly scented water are distributed around the table. The towels should be unfolded so that the steam gently bathes your face, and then you wash your face and hands with the towel. This ritual completes the dinner preparations, and now the food is brought to the table.

An average Japanese dinner always includes fish, rice, pickles, soup, dipping sauces, and green tea. Very formal meals can include as many as three soups and a dozen or more side dishes. I was once a guest for dinner in Japan for which an entire restaurant was taken over by my host for the evening. No one else could dine in the restaurant that night, and in the middle of the meal, between courses, Kabuki actors performed for us, and then the meal continued. Usually, however, all the food is brought to the table at once. The food is light, and moderate portions are encouraged, so it's easy to appreciate such a large selection. The soup is quite often miso, a soup made from a fish stock called dashi and soy bean paste. Miso is mild and yet simultaneously full-flavored, and contains bits of spring onion and white bean curd. Japanese rice is very fluffy and quite easy to pick up with chopsticks. The pickles are freshly marinated vegetables, and the side dishes include vegetable salads with sauces, sushi, and sashimi. Fish, meat, and poultry, plainly cooked, marinated, or deep-fried, are served with their own dipping sauces. One of my favorite eating experiences is to try a wide variety of sauces and marinades. In Japanese cooking, no mere sprinkling of salt or pepper will do. With just a few basic ingredients such as soy sauces, rice wine, Japanese sweetened vinegar, and soup stock, a generous number of sauces are prepared. You may use the sauces as generously or as sparingly as you wish.

The Japanese love to dress up food with special garnishes that reflect the season of the year. Symbolic or real leaves and flowers are typical. I once sampled a dish of quail eggs, still in the shell, presented on a plate, with delicate flowers entwined all around the eggs to form a frame. When I opened the eggs, I discovered that they held the finest caviar. The chef, unfortunately, wouldn't part with the secret of how he got the caviar inside the eggs without breaking the shells.

Additional charm comes to Japanese dining from the use of serving dishes which are individually designed for specific foods. Each lacquered china dish comes in a different size, shape, and color. Soup bowls have small rounded covers to keep liquid hot. Some containers look exactly like little jewelry boxes with matching lids. When all the dishes are arranged together on the table, the patterns and designs flow together to create an elegant setting.

Since sugar is used as a spice in many sauces, Japanese desserts are very light. Fresh fruits such as mandarin oranges or lichee nuts can provide the meal's finishing touch. You may prefer to serve either ice cream or sherbet. A wide choice of beverages may also be presented. Traditional drinks include warmed sake served in individual flasks with small cups, plain green tea, beer, and plum wine.

The following recipes, all for dishes that I thoroughly enjoy, will help you create a Japanese evening at home.

Japanese Glossary

Dashi	fish soup (stock)
Gohan	plain steamed rice. (*Gohan* literally translated means "honorable food.")
Katsuobushi	dried bonito fish. (Flaked dried bonito fish is *hanagatsuo*.)
Kombu	kelp (seaweed)
Matcha	green tea powder
Mirin	sweetened rice wine, used only for cooking. (An acceptable substitute is sherry and sugar, 4 parts sherry to 1 part sugar.)
Miso	soybean paste
Nigiri zushi (sushi)	filets of raw fresh fish served on flavored rice with *wasabi*
Sake	rice wine
Sashimi	slices of fresh raw fish
Shoga	fresh ginger root. (Can be preserved in dry sherry and will then last one year.)
Shabu-shabu	method of cooking beef and vegetables in broth at the table
Shoyu	Japanese soy sauce in both a light variety, for soups and sauces, and a dark variety, for marinades and sauces. Soy sauces contain salt.
Spring onion	scallion
Su	rice vinegar (very mild). (A substitute would be ¼ cup white wine vinegar, plus ⅛ cup water.)

Sushi-su	preseasoned vinegar used only on sushi rice. You could substitute ¼ cup white wine vinegar, ⅛ cup water, 1 tablespoon sugar, and a dash of salt, well blended
Tempura	method of cooking pieces of seafood and vegetables coated with a light batter and deep-fried
Teriyaki	marinated and broiled chicken, fish, or beef
Tofu	soybean curd
Tsukemono	pickles
Wasabi	hot green "mustard" (made from powdered horseradish and water)
Yakitori	marinated, skewered broiled chicken

Note: Any ingredients not carried in your local market or specialty food shop can be purchased by mail-order from the list of stores at the end of this book. Sake can be purchased at many liquor stores.

Dashi

Most Oriental stores sell dashi stock in a powdered form. If you purchase such a product, simply follow the package directions for a ready-made stock that doesn't need to be strained. To make a stock which is a bit more complex, follow the recipe below.

5–6 cups water
  ½ cup kombu (seaweed)

½ cup hanagatsuo (bonito flakes)

Bring the water to a boil. Add seaweed and simmer for 3–4 minutes. Add bonito flakes, and bring to a second boil. As soon as liquid starts to boil, remove from heat. Cool slightly and strain.

Miso Soup

This is also called bean soup, and it is probably the most popular Japanese soup served outside Japan.

5–6 cups dashi
  5 ounces tofu (bean curd)
  2 spring onions (scallions)
  1 slice fresh ginger (about the size of a quarter)

5 ounces red or white miso (soy bean paste)
Dash of light shoyu (soy sauce)

Put dashi into a soup pot. Cut tofu into ½″ squares. Chop spring onions into very small pieces. Bring dashi to a boil, then quickly reduce heat. Mince fresh ginger, and add to dashi. Remove a little hot stock, mix it with the miso, and then return the entire mixture to the soup pot. Stir, and add tofu, spring onion, and shoyu. Bring soup to boiling point, remove from heat immediately, and serve. (The miso will thicken slightly and settle from the dashi as the soup cools. This is normal; the miso is simply denser than the dashi.) *(Serves 4)*

Cabbage Pickles

Remember, Japanese "pickles" aren't at all like Western pickles. The following salted vegetable dish, however, is typical Japanese cooking and is served as a side dish at the beginning of a meal.

1 pound white cabbage	1 tablespoon sugar
2 spring onions	Juice from ½ fresh lemon
1 green pepper	½ teaspoon crushed red chili
½ cup su (vinegar)	pepper
¼ cup dark shoyu	

Shred the cabbage. Cut spring onions into ½″ long pieces. Remove seeds and veins from green pepper; cut into rings. Combine vegetables in a large bowl. Combine remaining ingredients to make a marinade. Pour marinade over vegetables. Cover with a dish which just fits inside the bowl and directly rests on the vegetables. Place a two-pound weight on the dish, and let stand for at least two hours. Drain marinade before serving.

Sautéed Bamboo Shoots

In this recipe, pea sprouts may be substituted for bamboo shoots. These sprouts are larger than bean sprouts and can be purchased in most health food stores and Oriental vegetable stores.

2 tablespoons vegetable oil	3 tablespoons mirin or 2
2 cups drained bamboo shoots,	tablespoons sherry plus 1
sliced	teaspoon sugar
⅓ cup dark shoyu	

Heat the oil in a skillet. Sauté the bamboo shoots in the oil, stirring rapidly until the shoots are light brown. Reduce heat, and combine shoyu and mirin in a small bowl. Add liquid to the skillet, increase heat, and cook an additional two minutes. (If using sprouts, after adding the liquid simply stir the sprouts until they're coated with shoyu and mirin and serve at once.) *(Serves 4)*

Ginger Eggplant

This dish may be served as an appetizer or a side vegetable. It may also be served hot or cold.

1 large eggplant
½ teaspoon salt
½ cup dark shoyu
4 tablespoons mirin or 3
    tablespoons sherry plus 1
    teaspoon sugar

1 teaspoon shredded shoga
    (ginger—fresh is preferred)
    (or ¼ teaspoon of
    powdered ginger)

Peel the eggplant, and cut into circles ¼″ wide. Cut each circle into ¼″ wide strips. Sprinkle the strips with salt, and let stand for 30 minutes to draw out excess liquid. Drain strips after 30 minutes, and dry them well with paper towels. Place eggplant into a large bowl. Combine shoyu, mirin, and ginger. Pour sauce over eggplant, and marinate for 2–3 hours.

Preheat broiler. After the eggplant has marinated, place it with the marinade in a shallow pan. Broil for 5–7 minutes for firm eggplant or 12–15 minutes if you prefer it softer. *(Serves 4)*

Green Bean Salad

2 cups fresh green beans   ¼ cup shredded cooked pork
¼ cup light shoyu   1 tablespoon sesame seeds
3 tablespoons su

Steam green beans until tender. Set aside to cool. Combine shoyu and su. Pour liquid over beans; marinate one hour. Just before serving, drain off marinade. Top green beans with pork; sprinkle sesame seeds over the top of the salad, and serve. *(Serves 4)*

Spinach Roll

The following may be served as an appetizer or a side dish.

2 eggs   1 clove garlic
½ teaspoon sugar   2 tablespoons vegetable oil
1 teaspoon light shoyu   1 cup cooked spinach, finely
⅛ teaspoon freshly minced   chopped
   ginger or a pinch of   Shoyu for dipping
   powdered ginger

Beat eggs lightly with sugar and shoyu, add ginger and set aside. Cut garlic clove in half. Rub on half on the bottom of an omelette pan or small skillet. Discard used garlic half. Heat half the oil in the pan. Pour in half the egg mixture, turning pan so that the bottom is evenly covered with egg. Cook over low heat until the egg is set. Remove cooked egg from pan, and set aside. Cook remaining egg mixture in the same way, beginning with garlic. Arrange ½ cup spinach down the center of each omelette in a straight line. Roll up the omelettes around the spinach to form a cylinder. Slice each rolled omelette diagonally into several pieces. Serve with a small bowl of shoyu in which to dip the pieces of omelette. *(Serves 4)*

Gohan

I especially enjoy Koda rice and have found that if you have an upset stomach, eating Koda made with extra water will help relieve the discomfort. Once you begin cooking with different kinds of rice, you'll discover that each is unique and has its own individual texture and flavor. Koda, for instance, looks a bit like a bowl full of shiny small pearls, when cooked properly. After you've experimented with several varieties of Oriental rice, you'll decide which you like best.

In this recipe, the heat is turned up high for 10 seconds after the rice is cooked, and then the rice rests for 10 minutes before being served. This process is what gives Japanese style rice its special texture, which makes it so easy to pick up with chopsticks.

½ cup uncooked rice per person   1 cup water for every ½ cup of
                                                                              rice to be cooked

Note: If you're serving plain rice, with the sauces, you may add up to ¾ teaspoon salt for each cup of uncooked rice, if you wish.

Wash rice several times in cold running water, until water draining from rice runs clear. Set rice aside in colander to drain completely.

Measure rice and appropriate amount of water into a heavy saucepan with a tight-fitting lid. Cover saucepan, bring water to a boil quickly, lower heat, and simmer rice for about 20 minutes or until the water is completely absorbed. Then, leaving the lid on the pan, turn the heat high for 10 seconds, and remove the saucepan from the heat. Let the rice stand 10 minutes, then serve it in small individual bowls. (Note: You may wish to invest in a Japanese automatic rice cooker if you cook rice often.)

Sushi Rice

3 cups cooked rice	1 teaspoon sugar
2 tablespoons su	Dash of salt

While the rice is still warm, sprinkle it with a combination of su mixed with the sugar and dash of salt. Toss with chopsticks or wooden fork to distribute liquid evenly.

Note: You may also use sushi-su, preseasoned vinegar that you may purchase in specialty stores.

Nigiri Zushi (Sushi)

Generations ago, the Japanese fermented in salt the fish they used for sushi. Gradually, however, they have come to prefer fresh fish in this dish. When eating sushi, begin with the most mild fish and end with the more full-flavored fish. If you go to a Japanese restaurant, sit at the sushi bar, and let the chef help you with your selection. It's a wonderful way to spend an evening, and in no time at all your taste in sushi may even include more exotic items such as sea urchin and eel.

Nigiri means "hand-made." If you're hesitant to try sushi, just start out with the shrimp.

3 cups prepared sushi rice
12 large shrimps
36 slices of any of the following combination of raw fish fillets: (slices about 2" x 1" x ⅛") tuna, sea bass, abalone, yellow tail, squid, octopus, sea trout, or flounder

Wasabi (horseradish "mustard")
Thin slices of gari (pickled slices of ginger)
Dark shoyu

Prepare the sushi rice as directed in the previous recipe. Parboil the shrimp. Remove their shells, cut along the underside to open flat, clean, and devein. Prepare slices of whichever other fish you have selected. Squid or octopus should be in ¼" thick slices and should be dipped briefly into boiling water. All other fish should be completely uncooked.

For each slice of fish, take about 2 tablespoons of sushi rice, and shape it into an oblong about 2" x 1" x ½". (If the rice sticks to your hands, rinse your hands and then moisten them with plain water before you make each rice oblong. Experience will dictate how much water to use; too much will cause the rice grains to separate and you'll have to begin again. Use a clean, damp lint-free towel to reduce the moisture on your hands and practice, practice, practice.) Put a dab of wasabi onto one side of the fish, and then place the fish, wasabi side down, onto the rice. (Wasabi is sold in powdered form. Simply mix wasabi with water until it looks like a thick paste. Wasabi is strong, so don't overdo it. If you like the taste, you can always add some prepared wasabi into your own dish of soy sauce.) Prepare parboiled fish in the same manner. Serve with slices of pickled ginger and dark shoyu for dipping. (Dip the top of the fish into the sauce, since the rice tends to soak up too much.) Use chopsticks or just eat as finger food. *(Serves 4)*

Tempura

Tempura is a unique and wonderful way to prepare quick fried seafood and vegetables. The batter used is very light and crispy. The secret in preparing the batter is to use very cold water. If you let a few ice cubes melt in the water you use for the recipe, the batter should come out perfectly every time.

Step 1: Preparing the fish and vegetables

16 large shrimp	1 large green pepper
1 large sweet onion	1 small bunch broccoli
1 small eggplant	8 large fresh mushrooms
1 sweet potato	

Wash, shell, and devein shrimp. Peel onion and cut it into ¼″ slices. Cut eggplant into ¼″ slices. Cut sweet potato into ⅛″ slices. Remove seeds and veins from green pepper; slice into strips ½″ wide. Cut broccoli into small spears. Wash and dry mushrooms. Set these items aside.

Step 2: Preparing the deep fryer

Heat vegetable oil in a deep fat fryer to 350° F. The oil depth should be at least three inches.

Step 3: Preparing the batter while the oil heats

Tempura Batter

3 egg yolks°	2 cups flour (if available, use
2 cups very cold water	Japanese wheat flour)
	½ cup cornstarch

Always prepare tempura batter just before using it. Beat the egg yolks lightly in a large bowl. Add the cold water and mix well. Combine flour and cornstarch in a flour sifter; sift mixture into egg and water. Mix batter quickly so that it has a light, non-sticky consistency. Don't overmix; a few lumps of flour are quite acceptable.

°Egg whites may be frozen for use in other recipes.

Step 4: Cooking the tempura

Be sure that all the shrimp and vegetables are dry. Dip the mildest flavored vegetables into the batter first, coating each side well. Lower coated vegetables into the hot oil, cooking until light golden brown. Drain on paper towels, and keep all cooked tempura warm in a slightly heated oven while you cook the remaining ingredients. Serve with the following sauces for dipping. *(Serves 4)*

Tempura Sauces

Sesame Mirin Sauce

1 cup dashi

⅓ cup mirin (sweet rice cooking wine) or ⅓ cup sherry plus 2 tablespoons sugar

¼ cup light shoyu

½ teaspoon hot sesame oil

2 teaspoons sesame seeds

Combine dashi, mirin, shoyu, and hot sesame oil in a small bowl. Sprinkle sesame seeds on top.

Lemon Sake Sauce

¼ cup lemon juice (preferably fresh)

½ cup dark shoyu

½ cup sake (rice wine)

½ cup dashi

Combine all of the above in a small bowl.

Yakitori

This is barbequed chicken, Japanese style. Serve as an appetizer or main dish. In warm weather, yakitori can be cooked on an outdoor grill.

1 pound uncooked chicken
   filets
½ cup dry sherry
2 tablespoons sugar
½ cup dark shoyu
¼ cup vegetable oil
¼ teaspoon freshly minced
   ginger root, or dash of
   powdered ginger

1 garlic clove
⅛ teaspoon red chili peppers
   (flaked cayenne
   acceptable)
16 small white onions (cooked)
1 green pepper
8 skewers

Cut chicken into large bite-size pieces. Combine sherry, sugar, shoyu, oil, ginger, garlic, and chili pepper in a small bowl. Pour liquid over chicken, and allow to marinate for one hour. Meanwhile, peel and cook white onions. Remove veins and seeds from green pepper; cut pepper into large bite-size pieces. After chicken has marinated, preheat the broiler. While broiler heats, lightly oil skewers, and skewer chicken and vegetables. Broil for several minutes on each side until meat is cooked through. Baste with marinade during cooking process. *(Serves 4)*

Oyako Donburi

Beef, pork, or shrimp can be substituted for the chicken used in oyako donburi. This is a good way to use leftovers to yield a completely different dish. The beaten egg that is added at the end of the cooking process takes on a custardlike consistency and makes the texture of this dish highly unusual. Note that oyako donburi is served on hot rice; you can start cooking the rice first and then begin the donburi.

4 cups cooked hot rice	1 garlic clove
2 cups cooked chicken, cut into bite-size pieces	¼ cup onion, thinly sliced
1 cup chicken broth	¼ cup spring onion, in ½" pieces, green part included
¼ cup shoyu	1 cup sliced mushrooms
¼ cup sherry mixed with 1 tablespoon sugar	¼ teaspoon freshly squeezed lemon juice
1 slice (about 1" in diameter) fresh ginger, minced	2 medium eggs, at room temperature, beaten

Prepare the chicken, and set it aside. Combine broth, shoyu, sherry and sugar, ginger, garlic, and both kinds of onion in a saucepan. Bring to a boil, reduce heat, and simmer until vegetables are tender. Add chicken and mushrooms; stir and add lemon juice. Increase heat and, when sauce comes to a boil, add the beaten eggs, and stir one minute. Remove pan from heat, cover, and let stand 3–5 minutes. Divide cooked rice into 4 bowls; spoon oyako donburi over rice and serve. *(Serves 4)*

Teriyaki

When this dish is finished, the food will have a thick, rich brown glaze on each side. For best results, cook the meat under the broiler as far away from the heat as possible until the last few minutes. Then move the broiler tray up close to the heat.

2 pounds steak, chicken, or a
    rich fish such as tuna,
    mackerel, or salmon
½ cup dark shoyu
¼ cup sake
¼ cup dry sherry

2 tablespoons sugar
1 teaspoon freshly minced
    ginger root, or ¼ teaspoon
    powdered ginger
1 garlic clove

Wash and dry meat. Cut into 4 individual pieces. Combine shoyu, sake, sherry, sugar, ginger, and garlic in a small bowl. Pour liquid over meat in a large bowl, and allow to marinate for at least two hours. After meat has marinated, preheat broiler. Cook as directed above, basting frequently with marinade and turning individual pieces of meat during cooking process so that coating clings all over. *(Serves 4)*

Baked Salmon-Stuffed Squid

If you want to try a truly exotic baked salmon, purchase squid steaks about the size of a filet of sole. Take a double-edged knife, and cut through the length of the squid, leaving the two ends uncut so that a "tunnel" is formed. Put baby salmon filets inside the squid, and broil until the outside of the squid is lightly browned and the inside of the squid and the salmon are cooked through.

Baked Salmon

The following recipe is a particularly good way to serve salmon at parties, since it comes to the table wrapped up in a silver foil package. Also, preparation time is minimal, and the fish is cooked in twenty minutes.

4 squares of aluminum foil	4 slices of fresh lemon, peel
1 tablespoon vegetable oil	removed
4 salmon steaks	2 tablespoons dark shoyu
8 large fresh mushrooms	2 tablespoons mirin

Preheat oven to 350° F. Oil the aluminum foil squares. Wash and dry salmon steaks, and place individual steaks on oiled squares. Wash and dry mushrooms, and cut in half lengthwise. Peel and slice the fresh lemon, removing seeds. Combine shoyu and mirin in a cup. Sprinkle fish equally with shoyu/mirin mixture. Place 4 mushroom slices on each fish steak. Put a lemon slice on top of the mushrooms, and fold the foil closed, sealing well to prevent any juices from escaping. Bake for 20 minutes in preheated oven as directed above. Serve in the foil, and let each guest open his own surprise package. Serve with cooked rice. *(Serves 4)*

Shabu-shabu

Shabu-shabu is a communal meal cooked at the table. Everyone shares the same cooking pot and takes his food from the pot at a leisurely pace. This dish was originally a Mongolian specialty prepared with lamb and cooked in a heavy pot hung over an outdoor fire. To me, it seems a bit like a Japanese fondue.

1½ pounds lean beef, sliced into paper-thin 2″ squares	1 large block of tofu
5 cups chicken stock	8 leaves Chinese cabbage, cut into large pieces
4 spring onions	2 cups pea sprouts
8 large fresh mushrooms	1 cup bamboo shoots

Prepare beef slices. If meat is slightly frozen it will be easier to cut into paper-thin 2″ squares. Set meat slices aside. Put chicken stock into a large, heavy pot over a low flame. While stock heats, wash and dry spring onions; cut into 2″ pieces. Wash and dry mushrooms. Cut tofu into large bite-size pieces. Wash and dry cabbage, and cut into large pieces. Wash and drain pea sprouts. Slice bamboo shoots. Arrange meat and vegetables on a large platter. Set up a hot plate on your dining table. When the stock has reached the boiling point, place it on the hot plate, and call your guests to the table. Everyone can help himself to meat and vegetables, holding chosen pieces in the broth for a few moments until the food is cooked. It's also all right to cook all of the ingredients at once by simply sliding everything from the platter into the broth; then serve your guests the cooked food or let them help themselves. At the end of the meal, the remaining chicken broth should be divided evenly among your guests in small bowls. To add flavor to the main dish, serve the following sauce in which diners may dip the cooked meat and vegetables after removing them from the cooking pot. (*Serves 4*)

Shabu-shabu Dipping Sauce

1 cup chicken stock
¼ cup dark shoyu (may use
    more for a richer sauce)

1 tablespoon su
¼ teaspoon toasted crushed
    sesame seeds

Combine stock, shoyu, and su in a small bowl. Sprinkle sesame seeds on top.

Green Tea Ice Cream

Green tea ice cream has a delicate, subtle flavor, and resembles pistachio ice cream in color.

1 pint vanilla ice cream
¼ teaspoon vanilla extract

2–3 teaspoons matcha (powdered
    green tea)

Allow ice cream to soften at room temperature. Stir vanilla into softened ice cream. Gradually begin adding matcha, stirring well after each addition, until ice cream reaches desired taste. Refreeze ice cream. *(Serves 4)*

Gypsy Cuisine

Introduction

Gypsies are a breed apart. Like most independent people, they value their freedom and privacy above all else. Romantics would have you believe that the wandering gypsy's life is nothing but carefree irresponsibility. Critics claim that all gypsies transmute irresponsibility into thievery. Both views are inaccurate. Gypsies are certainly wanderers, but their nomadic lifestyle carries with it a full set of rules. And while they may on occasion sidestep an outsider's law, gypsies are always true to their own.

My mother was a gypsy, and I spent several of my teenage years traveling through France with a gypsy troupe. I worked as a minstrel, sang folk songs, and played my own guitar. My preparation for this job was entertaining in nightclubs when I was younger, and I still remember the magic moment when, at age twelve, I received my first paycheck.

People are always curious about gypsies, wanting to know who they are and where they came from. Gypsyologists have traced the origins of the gypsies back to northwest India. Exactly why they

55

left India is still a mystery, although perhaps gypsies merely chose to keep the reason a secret. One thing that's clear is that there are inherent difficulties in constantly moving from one place to another. Just think about the everyday chore of preparing meals. For most of us, even fixing food for a weekend camping trip is a challenge. Gypsy cooks, faced with cooking in a caravan, had to be among the world's most ingenious chefs. Before the days of modern trailers, replete with stoves and refrigerators, they cooked over campfires or, during cold and rainy weather, on potbellied stoves inside wagons or tents. They used reflector ovens for baking. Roasting was done on spits over an open fire. The menu always would change as the caravan crossed a border, since the gypsies daily purchased or traded for fresh produce. Gradually, their cuisine took on an international flavor as certain favorite dishes from one region were adapted to fit the ingredients on hand.

Gypsies have always favored soups and stews. These dishes are easy to make, and just about anything you put into either of them winds up tasting good. These marvelous concoctions also can be quite exotic. For instance, our gypsy recipe section includes directions for making dandelion soup with cream. The dandelion is a plant that deserves to be recognized as a delicacy. (Dandelion greens also can be sautéed in oil with a little flour, salt, and pepper.) If you'd rather start with a less exotic dish, begin with beef goulash, pork and sauerkraut ragout, or chicken paprika.

The foods mentioned so far are for everyday meals. What about cooking for special occasions? Perhaps the most joyous event for any traveler in a foreign country is meeting a friend from home. The natural inclination when such a reunion takes place is to have a celebration. Since a gypsy's home is wherever he happens to be, a celebration can take place anywhere at any time. And because friends are worthy of honor, a gypsy spares no expense and effort to make sure his guest feels welcome. "*Patshiv*" in the gypsy language, Romany, means ceremonial celebration. Among the requirements for an ideal patshiv are a warm summer night with cooling breezes, a grassy meadow with a sweetwater brook for a border, crackling campfires with a huge reserve of cut firewood, and a squad of violin and guitar players with nimble fingers—not to mention lavish amounts of food. The aromas of rich hunter's steak and wild goose seasoned with sage, thyme, and marjoram waft through the air. Succulent baked zucchini chicken adds its fragrance to piping hot red cabbage cooked with apples. Potatoes baked with sausage are displayed next to rabbit stew in a thick gravy. Pickled eggplant, cucumbers with yogurt, and brandied pears with apricots vie for your attention. Fill any empty spaces on your plate with black olives, tomatoes, onions, red peppers, and salads. You don't have to sample everything at once; a patshiv can last for several days.

As the evening wears on, someone will hum the melody of a folk song, and, before you know it, everyone will join in, and the campfires will be surrounded by whirling dancers. A storyteller will be moved to speak of her ancestors, and new legends will be born before the night retreats from the sun. Dawn will finally make an entrance accompanied by the echoes of an epic song composed just for the guest of honor. You'll fall asleep believing that the romantic view of a gypsy's life isn't so far from the truth.

The gypsies like to remember their ancestors and departed relatives and friends. They always toast to the past and the memory of these people, and then pour a little wine onto the ground or sprinkle a few drops into the air. They do this so that their ancestors' spirits can participate in the toast and in the atmosphere of the patshiv. Gypsies and their spirits also favor drinking cold clear water, beer, brandy, and very strong black coffee.

We invite you to a patshiv through the recipes that follow.

Hummus

Hummus is one of those wonderful appetizers that can quickly turn into a full-course meal. Try serving fresh vegetables along with warm pita bread to scoop up this dip. Also serve warm ripe olives and Feta or Bryndza cheese on the side.

2 cups cooked chick peas
½ cup liquid from peas
⅔ cup sesame butter (available at health food stores)
½–¾ cup fresh lemon juice (to taste)

1 garlic clove
½ teaspoon salt
¼ teaspoon cayenne pepper
Fresh parsley

Combine chick peas, liquid from the peas, sesame butter, lemon juice, garlic, salt, and cayenne in a blender or food processor. Blend mixture until it's very smooth. Pour into a bowl, and garnish with fresh parsley. Serve as suggested above. *(Serves 8 as appetizer)*

Pickled Eggplant

Pickled eggplant, cucumbers with yogurt, and pickled cucumbers can be served as side dishes or salads with any of the main dishes in the Gypsy section.

1 medium-size eggplant
1 ripe tomato, chopped
1 small onion, chopped
1 garlic clove

3 tablespoons olive oil
2 tablespoons vinegar
Salt and pepper

Cut unpeeled eggplant in half lengthwise and broil for 12–15 minutes, or until pulp is quite soft and cooked through. Cool eggplant, and remove pulp from peel with a large spoon. Discard peel. Combine eggplant with chopped tomato and chopped onion in a medium-size bowl. Combine garlic with olive oil and vinegar in a small jar; shake well and pour over vegetables. Mix well, season to taste with salt and pepper, and chill. *(Serves 4)*

Cucumbers with Yogurt

1 large cucumber
½ cup plain yogurt
¼ teaspoon salt

Dash of cayenne pepper (or
    more, to taste)
¼ teaspoon dill

Peel cucumber and cut into thin slices. Put slices into medium-size bowl. Combine yogurt with salt and pepper; add to cucumber slices and stir well. Just before serving, sprinkle dill on top. *(Serves 4)*

Pickled Cucumbers

1 large cucumber
1 small onion
¼ cup apple cider vinegar
¼ teaspoon salt

¾ teaspoon sugar
¼ teaspoon crushed red chili
    pepper (or less, to taste)

Peel cucumber and onion; slice both into thin slices, and put slices into medium-size bowl. Combine vinegar, salt, and sugar. Pour over cucumber and onion. Sprinkle chili pepper on top. Chill and allow to marinate several hours; the flavor becomes stronger as the vegetables marinate. *(Serves 4)*

Dandelion Soup

The next time you're wondering what to do with all the dandelions growing in your lawn, pick some of the leaves, and use them for this delicious soup. The new small leaves will have the most delicate flavor.

Young nettle leaves may be substituted for dandelions and make a fine soup; however, wear gloves while picking them as the stems have an oil that may make your skin sting.

6 cups chicken stock	1 cup fresh mushrooms
4 cups dandelion leaves, from young plants	½ cup heavy cream
	½ cup sour cream
4 small white potatoes	4 tablespoons butter
2 carrots	¼ teaspoon salt (or to taste)
1 stalk celery	Black pepper
4 leeks, white part only (whites of scallions may be used)	

Bring stock to a boil in a large soup kettle. Wash dandelion leaves, and add them to the stock. Cover and simmer 30 minutes. Remove from heat, cool, and strain stock. Discard the leaves. Put stock back into the kettle, and simmer until it reaches the boiling point. While stock simmers, peel and slice potatoes, carrots, and celery into thin slices. Cut leeks into ¼″ slices. When stock begins to boil, add vegetables; cover and simmer for one hour. After one hour, wash and dry mushrooms; cut into slices, and add to the soup. Simmer 10 minutes, then add both of the creams and the butter. Stir until butter has melted and soup is heated through. Add salt to taste, and serve. Garnish with black pepper—freshly ground preferred. *(Serves 4–6)*

Fish Chowder

This soup can be served hot or cold. If you serve it chilled, provide your guests with small bowls of sliced cucumber, sour cream, dill, fresh parsley, and thin slices of fresh lemon to use as condiments.

6 cups chicken stock	1 tablespoon sugar
3 carrots	2 tablespoons vinegar
1 turnip	1 2-pound sea bass, sea trout,
1 large onion	ocean perch, or red
2 stalks celery	snapper, cleaned and
1 clove garlic, crushed	scaled
2 bay leaves	2 cups shredded white cabbage
12 black peppercorns	2 fresh tomatoes, cut into
	chunks
	Salt and pepper

Pour stock into a large soup pot, and slowly bring to boil. While stock heats, peel carrots, turnip, and onion. Cut these vegetables and the celery into thin slices. When stock reaches boiling point, add sliced vegetables, crushed garlic clove, bay leaves, and peppercorns to the pot. Reduce heat, and simmer for one hour. Next add sugar and vinegar to the soup. Stir, and then add the cleaned, scaled fish (head and tail should remain intact, but you can remove them if you wish). Cover and simmer 20 minutes. Remove fish, and add cabbage to the soup. When fish is cool enough to handle, remove skin, head, tail, and all bones. Put fish pieces back into the soup, add tomatoes, and simmer 10 minutes. Season to taste with salt and pepper. *(Serves 4–6)*

Green Beans with Sour Cream

4 cups green beans	2 teaspoons fresh chopped
4 tablespoons butter	sweet basil (or ½ teaspoon
2 small garlic cloves, crushed	dried sweet basil)
1 medium onion, thinly sliced	Dash of black pepper, salt to
1 large tomato, chopped	taste
	1 cup sour cream

Steam green beans until tender, and then remove from heat. (You may use frozen beans; just follow package directions for cooking.) In a large skillet, melt butter. Sauté thinly sliced onion and crushed garlic in butter until onion is transparent. Remove and discard garlic, then add tomato, basil, pepper, and salt. Simmer until vegetables are soft and cooked through—about 5 minutes. Add cooked green beans, heat through, and add sour cream. Stir well to blend cream and vegetables. When sauce begins to bubble, serve at once. *(Serves 4–6)*

Red Cabbage with Apples

1 medium-size red cabbage	½ cup plus 2 tablespoons water
2 apples (MacIntosh apples are	1 tablespoon vinegar
good)	1 teaspoon sugar
3 tablespoons butter	1 bay leaf
1 medium onion, chopped	1 teaspoon caraway seeds

Shred the cabbage. Peel and core apples; slice thinly. Melt butter in a large saucepan. Add onion and sauté until onion is transparent. Add cabbage and sliced apples to the saucepan. Mix together water, vinegar, and sugar. Pour over the cabbage, and add bay leaf and caraway seeds. Cover saucepan and reduce heat. Simmer slowly for 45 minutes. *(Serves 4–6)*

Potatoes with Sausage

This dish combines meat, potatoes, and vegetables. It's a good meal to serve during the week if you haven't much time to prepare a hearty dinner. The paprika I use is medium-hot strength. Paprika varies from mild to medium-hot to hot, and you notice the subtle differences in spiciness only after you swallow! The hot paprika is not the same type of hot associated with chili peppers; it's a much less spicy flavor. Most paprika sold in supermarkets is mild; for a greater variety, visit a spice shop or purchase from a mail-order supplier.

8 large potatoes	4 tablespoons butter
3 large ripe tomatoes	2 cups water (more or less,
2 pounds thick link sausage	depending on size of
(cooked)	skillet)
1 large onion	2 teaspoons paprika
1 green pepper	1 teaspoon salt
1 stalk celery	½ teaspoon black pepper

Peel and thinly slice potatoes. Chop tomatoes. Cut sausage into ¼" slices. Peel onion, and chop into small pieces. Remove veins and seeds from green pepper; chop in small pieces. Chop celery. Melt butter in a large skillet. Sauté onion, pepper, and celery. When the onion is transparent, add the potatoes, tomatoes, and enough water to cover the potatoes. Add spices, and stir to blend. Cover skillet and cook 25–30 minutes over low heat until potatoes are almost cooked through. (Add more water if necessary.) When potatoes are almost done, add sausage slices and cook about 5 minutes, until sausage is heated through and potatoes are done. *(Serves 6)*

Beef Goulash

The surprise ingredient in my version of this traditional recipe is
beer. For a sweeter taste, omit the green pepper.

3 tablespoons vegetable oil
1 clove garlic
1½ pounds boneless chuck, in
    small chunks
4 small onions, cut in half
1 tablespoon paprika
⅔ cup beer
1 cup beef stock

1 green pepper
4 medium potatoes
2 tablespoons tomato paste
2 tomatoes, chopped
1 teaspoon sugar
1 tablespoon vinegar
    Salt and pepper

Heat vegetable oil in large saucepan or Dutch oven. Sauté garlic
in hot oil; remove garlic, and add meat to the pot, browning pieces
on all sides. Add onions, and sprinkle paprika over meat. Add beer
and stock, cover and simmer for 1 hour and 15 minutes. While meat
is simmering, remove seeds and veins from green pepper. Cut
pepper into wide strips. Peel potatoes and cut into quarters. (If you
use new potatoes, leave the skins on them.) Add pepper, potatoes,
tomato paste, chopped tomatoes, sugar, and vinegar to the pot.
Simmer uncovered until the potatoes are done. Season to taste with
salt and pepper. *(Serves 4)*

Chicken Paprika

I love this dish served with dumplings. (Recipe for Corn Dumplings follows.)

5 tablespoons butter	3 tablespoons tomato paste
2 medium onions, chopped	1 tablespoon paprika
3 pounds chicken, in pieces	12 black peppercorns
2 cups chicken stock	½ teaspoon salt
1 green pepper, chopped	1 cup sour cream
2 tomatoes, chopped	

Melt the butter in a Dutch oven. Sauté the chopped onions in the butter until the onions are transparent. Add the chicken pieces and brown on all sides. Add chicken stock, chopped green pepper, tomatoes, tomato paste, paprika, peppercorns, and salt. Cover the Dutch oven, and simmer chicken for one hour. Just before serving, stir in sour cream, and heat until dish is warmed through. *(Serves 4)*

Corn Dumplings

Both beef goulash and chicken paprika may be served with dumplings. If you cook dumplings with the beef you may eliminate the potatoes, if you wish. If you cook dumplings with the chicken, serve the sour cream in a separate bowl on the table instead of using it during the chicken paprika cooking process.

1½ cups water	2 teaspoons baking powder
½ teaspoon salt	¼ teaspoon black pepper
½ cup corn meal	1 egg
1 cup flour	

Combine water and salt in a medium-size saucepan. Bring water to a boil, then reduce heat so that the water is simmering. Slowly add corn meal, stirring constantly so mixture remains smooth. Continue to stir until corn meal is cooked and has thickened (the mixture will look like hot cooked cereal), then remove mixture from heat, and cool. Add flour, baking powder, and pepper to the cooled corn meal. Mix well, add the egg, and mix well again to form a batter. Drop the dumpling batter by large spoonfuls onto the top of the goulash or chicken after the meat is cooked. Cover and simmer for 15–20 minutes, or until the dumplings are cooked through. These dumplings are very light in texture and are truly delicious. *(Serves 4)*

Asparagus Fritters

These fritters are an unusual side dish and may be substituted for rice or potatoes in any meal. The texture of the cooked fritter is similar to a vegetable dumpling. If you like, another vegetable may be used instead of asparagus. For best results, cook the fritters in a 10″ cast iron skillet. This recipe makes twelve fritters, approximately 3 inches across.

1 scant cup flour (a little less than a full cup)
1 teaspoon baking powder
¼ teaspoon salt
½ cup plus 7 teaspoons milk
1 beaten egg

1 tablespoon melted butter
1 heaping cup cooked asparagus, cut into 1″ pieces
Vegetable oil

Sift together flour, baking powder, and salt into a large mixing bowl. Add milk, beaten egg, and melted butter, and stir until batter is very smooth. Add asparagus and stir gently until asparagus is well-coated with batter. Pour vegetable oil into a large 10″ cast iron skillet to a depth of ⅛ inch. Allow batter to rest while oil heats. (The oil is the right temperature when a bit of batter dropped into it immediately cooks and turns light brown.) When oil is heated, use a large spoon to pour the batter for each fritter into the pan. Fry three fritters at a time, turning each one only once when the first side is golden brown. Drain cooked fritters on paper towel while you fry the rest of the batter. *(Serves 4)*

Pork and Sauerkraut Ragout

This is another one-dish main meal that is made in a Dutch oven. I like the way the flavors blend together and yet still remain separate and distinctive. Pork and sauerkraut ragout is wonderful served over hot buttered noodles.

1½–2 pounds pork shoulder
  2 tablespoons vegetable oil
  1 large onion
  1 garlic clove
  1 tablespoon paprika

¼ teaspoon salt
1 teaspoon caraway seeds
½ cup water
1 cup beer
1½ pounds sauerkraut, drained
1 cup sour cream

Trim excess fat off pork, and cut the meat into small pieces. It's all right to cook this dish with pork bones included; they should be discarded before serving, but they add flavor to sauce. Set the pork aside, and heat the vegetable oil in a Dutch oven. While the oil heats, peel and chop the onion. Sauté the onion and garlic clove in the vegetable oil until the onions are transparent. Remove the garlic, add the pork, and brown well on all sides. Add paprika, salt, caraway seeds, water, and beer to the Dutch oven. Cover, cook for one hour, periodically skimming fat from the top of the sauce. After one hour of cooking, add drained sauerkraut, cover, and cook another 45 minutes. Garnish with sour cream. *(Serves 4)*

Lamb/Lima Stew

Lima beans replace potatoes in this hearty dish cooked with chicken stock for extra richness. The stew can be served for special occasions if you purchase loin chops and cut them into chunks; with a crisp salad and warm crusty bread you'll create a gourmet presentation.

2 tablespoons butter
2 garlic cloves
3 pounds lamb stew meat, with bones, in chunks
2 cups chicken stock
1 cup thinly sliced fresh carrots
1 cup dried lima beans
2½ cups ripe fresh tomatoes, coarsely chopped (about 3 medium tomatoes)

16 small white onions, outer skin removed
1 bay leaf
½ teaspoon paprika
1 tablespoon fresh parsley, finely minced
Salt and pepper
1 cup sour cream (optional)

Melt butter in a large stew pot that has a tightly fitting cover. When butter has melted, crush garlic cloves and sauté them until brown; remove sautéed garlic and discard. Add lamb and brown well on each side. Add stock, carrots, and lima beans; cover and simmer for one hour over low heat. Add fresh tomatoes, onion, bay leaf, and paprika, cover once more and continue cooking another 30 minutes. Sprinkle fresh parsley over top and serve with salt and pepper for individual seasoning; garnish with sour cream if desired. *(Serves 4)*

Hunter's Steak

This dish is made with venison or beef, with the cut of your choice. The vinegar tenderizes the meat and makes it delicious.

2 cups fresh carrots	½ teaspoon paprika
1 large onion	½ teaspoon mustard
4 tablespoons vegetable oil	Salt and pepper
2 pounds venison or beef steak	2 tablespoons flour
2 cups hot beef stock	4 tablespoons water
3 tablespoons vinegar	

Peel the carrots, and cut them into thin slices. Cook them in a small saucepot in enough water to just cover the carrots, or you may steam them in a vegetable steamer. Set aside cooked carrots. Peel and slice the onion. Heat the vegetable oil in a large skillet, and sauté the onions until they are transparent. Remove the onions, and add the meat to the skillet. Brown the meat on both sides, and then add hot beef stock, vinegar, paprika, and mustard to the skillet. Add the onions and simmer about 35–40 minutes, or until the meat is very tender. Season sauce to taste with salt and pepper. Combine flour and water to make a paste. Remove meat from the skillet and set it aside. Bring sauce to boil, and gradually add flour and water mixture to the sauce, stirring rapidly to thicken the sauce and make a gravy. Reduce heat, return the meat and the cooked carrots to the gravy, simmer gently to heat through and serve. *(Serves 4)*

Zucchini Chicken

This dish blends chicken with vegetables to produce a hearty meal with its own rich, flavorful broth which may be thickened with flour and water to make a gravy.

2 pounds chicken, in serving
    pieces
½ teaspoon salt
⅛ teaspoon black pepper
½ teaspoon paprika
2 medium tomatoes
1 medium onion

1 pound zucchini
1 cup chicken stock
1 tablespoon fresh oregano (or
    ½ teaspoon dried oregano)
2 tablespoons flour
4 tablespoons water

Preheat broiler. Wash and dry chicken pieces. Combine salt, pepper, and paprika. Sprinkle spices evenly over chicken. Broil chicken for 15 minutes, turning once. While chicken broils, chop tomatoes, peel onion and cut into thin slices, and cut zucchini into ½″ slices. Remove chicken from broiler and place in a large baking dish. Reduce oven to 350° F. Arrange vegetables on top of chicken, pour chicken stock into baking dish and sprinkle oregano over the top of the vegetables. Bake for one hour. If you wish to make a gravy, when chicken is cooked remove chicken and vegetables from the baking dish and place them onto a serving platter. Pour chicken broth into a small saucepan and bring to a boil. Mix flour with water to make a paste. Add the paste to the broth gradually while stirring rapidly, until gravy reaches desired thickness. *(Serves 4)*

Rabbit Stew

Although the citizens of ancient Greece believed that eating rabbit caused insomnia, the Romans were positive that eating rabbit for seven days in a row cured ugliness. In any case, it's a very tasty dish. Rabbit can be purchased frozen in many major supermarkets. Since it has little natural fat, rabbit is usually cooked with pork or bacon.

6 slices bacon or ¼ pound ground pork sausage	¼ teaspoon caraway seeds
	¼ teaspoon salt
1 large onion, sliced thinly	⅛ teaspoon black pepper
1 garlic clove	5 potatoes
2½ pounds rabbit meat, in pieces	2 carrots
1 cup beer	3 tablespoons flour
1 cup chicken stock	6 tablespoons water
½ teaspoon tarragon	

Fry bacon or sausage till done in a Dutch oven. Remove cooked meat (reheat for next day's breakfast). Sauté onion and garlic in the remaining fat, and then add the rabbit pieces, cooking on each side till lightly browned. While rabbit cooks, combine beer, stock, and seasonings. Peel potatoes and cut into quarters; cut carrots into pieces no thicker than ½ inch. Add beer, stock, seasonings, and vegetables to Dutch oven. Cover, reduce heat, and simmer for one hour or until vegetables are tender and rabbit is cooked through. Combine flour and water together to make a paste; add to the broth in the Dutch oven after the stew is cooked until the broth thickens to gravy. (As with all gravies, bring broth to a boil first and stir constantly as you add the flour-water mixture so that lumps don't form. Thicken according to taste.) *(Serves 4–6)*

Roast Goose

A goose has a larger amount of fat under its skin than other fowl. To render the fat, preheat your oven to 425° F. and when the goose is placed into the oven reduce the temperature to 325° F. for roasting. Also, lightly prick the bird's skin all over to allow the melting fat to drain from the goose as it cooks.

Pick a goose that weighs about 10 pounds; a bird weighing more may not be as tender. Roast the bird 15-20 minutes per pound, allowing an extra half-hour for cooking when the goose is stuffed. *(A 10-pound goose serves 4-6.)*

Preparation:

Wash and dry a 10-pound goose. Lightly prick the skin all over with a sharp fork (do not pierce meat, or you will lose juices). Rub a combination of 1 teaspoon sage, 1 teaspoon thyme, and 1 teaspoon marjoram over the outside and inside of the goose. Stuff with dressing (recipe on next page), and close the cavity by securing the skin with poultry skewers. Place the goose onto a roasting rack inside a large roasting pan. After the first hour of roasting, drain off the fat which has accumulated in the bottom of the roasting pan, and put ½ cup hot water into the bottom of the pan. Continue roasting until done, for a total of approximately 3½-4 hours if the bird is stuffed.

Dressing for Roast Goose

¼ pound butter
1 medium onion, chopped
1 stalk celery, chopped
½ pound ground pork sausage
6 cups dry bread cubes
2 medium apples
1 cup currants
¼ teaspoon salt

¼ teaspoon sage
¼ teaspoon marjoram
¼ teaspoon thyme
⅛ teaspoon black pepper
1 egg
¼ cup milk, goose stock, or
    chicken broth

Melt butter in a large skillet. Add chopped onions and celery and gently sauté until onion is transparent. Remove from heat and set aside. Sauté pork sausage in a medium skillet, drain fat, remove from heat, and set aside. Put dry bread into a large bowl. Peel, core, and chop apples. Add apples, currants, cooked onion, and celery with melted butter, drained cooked sausage, and all spices to the bread. Mix well. Beat the egg with the milk or stock or broth and add to the dressing. Mix well again and put the dressing into the goose.

Goose Stock and Gravy

If you wish to serve gravy with the roast goose, combine the following stock with the pan drippings, and thicken the mixture with a flour and water paste, as directed below.

Giblets and wing tips from
    goose
1 celery stalk, with top
1 large onion
2 carrots
6 peppercorns

¾ teaspoon rosemary
5 cups water
2 tablespoons flour plus 4
    tablespoons water
Salt and pepper

Place giblets into a medium saucepan. Cut celery into several pieces. Peel onion and cut in half. Cut carrots into several pieces. Add vegetables to saucepan. Add peppercorns, rosemary, and water to pan. Simmer gently until liquid reduces to about 3 cups. Strain and put liquid back into pan. Add pan drippings. Make a paste with the flour and water. Bring stock to boil, gradually add flour and water mixture, and stir rapidly until gravy has thickened. Season to taste with salt and pepper. *(Serves 4–6)*

Spiced Applesauce

I think it's good to serve unusual combinations from time to time to make a meal more interesting. The following recipe brings together freshly made applesauce and freshly grated horseradish for a sweet and sassy relish to serve as an accompaniment to meat and poultry dishes. Since preserved horseradish quite often has vinegar added to it, this should be made with fresh horseradish, available in most specialty stores. This recipe makes approximately 3 cups.

4 large green cooking apples
(Granny Smith are very
good)
1 cup water
½ cup sugar

¼ teaspoon vanilla extract
1 teaspoon freshly grated
horseradish (more or less
to taste)

Peel, core, and slice apples into fairly thin slices. Place into saucepan, add water, and bring to boil over moderate heat. Reduce heat so that mixture simmers, add sugar, stir, and cover saucepan. Simmer covered for 25 minutes, or until all of the apples are very soft. Remove from heat, cool slightly, and add vanilla. Purée with a beater or in a food processor. Put applesauce into a bowl and add horseradish. Chill before serving. *(Serves 4–6)*

Apricots and Pears in Brandy

This dish may be served on the side with roast goose or at the end of the meal as dessert. I like brandied fruit over ice cream or custard. If stored in a cool place, the fruit will keep for weeks. It will ferment as time passes and will become quite strong.

3 large ripe pears	2 cups sugar
2 cups ripe apricots	2 cups brandy

Peel and core the pears. Cut into thin slices. Remove pits from apricots and cut apricots into quarters. Mix sugar and brandy together until sugar is almost dissolved. Put fruit into a large glass jar with a close-fitting lid. Pour brandy mixture over the fruit and let stand overnight before serving. *(Serves 6–8)*

Spice Cake

This cake has two surprise ingredients that make it special: apple-sauce and natural apple juice.

1⅔ cups flour	⅓ cup brown sugar, loosely
¼ teaspoon baking powder	packed
1 teaspoon baking soda	⅓ cup melted butter
½ teaspoon salt	1 egg
¾ teaspoon cinnamon	⅓ cup natural apple juice
¼ teaspoon allspice	1 cup applesauce
1 cup sugar	1 cup raisins

Preheat oven to 350° F. Grease and flour a 9" x 9" x 2" pan; set aside. Sift together flour, baking powder, soda, salt, cinnamon, and allspice into a large bowl. Add sugars. Pour melted butter into a small bowl. Beat the egg and mix it into the butter. Stir apple juice into butter-egg mixture, and gradually add liquid to flour mixture. Stir well, add applesauce, stir again, and add raisins. Pour batter into pan and bake for 50–55 minutes, or until a toothpick inserted into the center of the cake comes out clean. *(Serves 4–6)*

Dessert Pancakes

These are thin pancakes, not unlike crepes. I like them sprinkled with confectioner's sugar or garnished with raspberry jam.

2 eggs, at room temperature	2 tablespoons sugar
¾ cup milk, at room temperature	½ teaspoon vanilla extract
	¼ teaspoon cinnamon
1 cup flour	8 teaspoons butter

Beat eggs and combine with milk in a large bowl. Add flour, sugar, vanilla, and cinnamon. Mix well to form a thin batter. For each pancake, melt 1 teaspoon butter in a 7″ skillet and add enough batter to the skillet to just cover the bottom. Turn the pancake only once, when the first side is lightly browned. Serve with choice of jams and confectioner's sugar. *(Serves 4)*

Poppy-seed Cookies

1 cup butter	⅛ teaspoon salt
½ cup sugar	¼ cup ground poppyseeds
2 eggs	¼ teaspoon cinnamon
½ teaspoon vanilla extract	¾ cup sweet chocolate morsels
2 cups sifted flour	2 tablespoons heavy cream

Melt butter in a small saucepan. Put melted butter into a large bowl and add sugar. Mix well. Beat eggs with vanilla; add to bowl, and mix well. Put flour in sifter; add salt. Gradually add sifted flour and salt to mixture in bowl. Add poppyseeds and cinnamon. Mix once more and form a ball of dough. Place dough in refrigerator and chill 2–3 hours. Preheat oven to 375° F. Shape 1″ balls of dough and place on greased cookie sheet 1″ apart. Make slight depression in the center of each ball. Bake in preheated oven for 15 minutes or until browned on bottom and lightly browned on top. While cookies are baking, melt chocolate morsels in the top of a double boiler. After the chocolate melts, stir in 2 tablespoons of heavy cream. Remove cookies from oven and allow to cool. Put a generous amount of melted chocolate on top of each cookie. Serve after chocolate has hardened. *(Makes about 40 cookies)*

Poppy-seed Honey Cakes

These are wonderful as dessert or with breakfast. I like them baked in a 9″ pie plate because it holds the dough in an even form.

Filling:

½ cup sweet butter	1 egg
½ cup plus 1 tablespoon honey	½ cup raisins
¼ cup milk	½ cup chopped walnuts
½ cup heavy cream	⅛ teaspoon salt
2 cups ground poppyseeds	½ teaspoon cinnamon
½ cup packed brown sugar	1 tablespoon lemon juice

In a large bowl, cream together butter and honey. Add remaining ingredients in order, stirring well after each addition. Transfer filling to a large saucepan. Cook about 30 minutes, until filling thickens, remove from heat, and set aside.

Dough:

3 envelopes dry yeast	¾ cup melted sweet butter
½ cup warm water	1 teaspoon vanilla extract
2 tablespoons sugar	3 medium eggs
⅓ cup sugar	5 cups flour
¾ cup milk	

Mix yeast, water, and 2 tablespoons sugar together in a small bowl; set aside for 10 minutes. In the meantime, combine ⅓ cup sugar with the milk, melted butter, and vanilla in a large bowl. Beat the eggs and add them to the bowl; stir well. Add the yeast mixture after it has rested for the 10 minutes mentioned above. Gradually add 2 cups of the flour, mixing well. Gradually add the rest of the flour until a smooth but pliable dough is formed. Turn the dough out onto a well-floured board, and knead for about 10 minutes. Form into a single ball, and place in a large buttered bowl. Spread a little bit of butter on top of the dough so it won't dry. Cover the bowl and place in a warm, draft-free spot until dough has doubled in size—about 1½ hours. Punch dough down and knead briefly, then divide into two equal portions. Roll each portion out on a lightly floured board into a rectangle about ¼" thick. Spread the filling evenly over each rectangle to within ½" from the edges, and then roll up the rectangles like jelly rolls. Bend rolled dough into a circular shape and seal edges together. Place cakes on a large, lightly buttered baking sheet or put each cake into a buttered 9" pie plate. Let rise until almost doubled in size, about one hour. Preheat oven to 350° F. while cakes rise; bake for 40–45 minutes, and remove when cakes are golden brown. (For a shiny surface, brush with a beaten egg mixed with one tablespoon of milk before putting into the oven.) *(Makes 2 cakes)*

Orange Icing

This is a thin, not-too-sweet icing that you can drizzle onto the top of the honey cakes, after the cakes cool.

⅔ cup confectioner's sugar
1 tablespoon plus 1 teaspoon
   milk
¼ teaspoon vanilla extract

1 teaspoon fresh orange juice
1 teaspoon finely grated orange
   rind, orange part (zest) only

Combine sugar, milk, vanilla, and orange juice in a small bowl. Mix well and add orange rind. Stir and drizzle onto cake.

Swiss Cuisine

Introduction

Nothing seems to promote hearty appetites quite like crisp, clean mountain air. In Switzerland, where air has no choice but to be crisp and clean (the Alps do not permit otherwise), it's easy to develop a very hearty appetite. The Swiss, wise and civilized people, have come up with a number of unique recipes which satisfy rigorous culinary demands. Not only are their traditional foods simple and elegant, but they also are easy to prepare, and they get the cook out of the kitchen quickly.

For one particular dish, the kitchen is, in essence, brought directly to the dining table. What is this magic dish? It is, of course, a fondue. I inherited the Swiss part of my genes from my father, and any fondue meal is among my favorites as it was among his. Imagine, for instance, golden melted cheese mixed with white wine simmering gently in a miniature cauldron set over a small flame on the table directly in front of you. Spear a bite-size piece of French bread or crisp apple slice with your small fondue fork, and dip it into the pot. Cover the "dunkable" with melted cheese, and pop it into your waiting mouth. That's surely one of the world's finest taste treats! And you get an extra bonus with a cheese fondue. It's "la réligièuse," the crusty layer of cooked cheese that gathers on the bottom of the pot. Some people insist it's the best part of the whole meal.

Meat and seafood are also used for fondues. For cooking these foods, the pot is filled with hot vegetable oil. Any number of dipping sauces and a fresh salad round out the menu. Be forewarned that if you lose a dunkable in the fondue pot, you'll have to pay a penalty. Unwritten law has it that a woman must kiss her partner and a man must supply extra wine for the table. Not surprisingly, many diners have devised original ways to lose dunkables at opportune moments.

Whenever a Swiss recipe calls for cheese, make an effort to use a cheese from Switzerland. Cooking with naturally genuine aged Swiss cheese will give the dish you've chosen a richer flavor than you'll get from most domestic varieties. Switzerland is dotted with family-owned dairies which provide the milk for over one hundred different types of cheeses. The Swiss, who know a good thing when they taste it, don't export all of these special dairy products. Some varieties of local Swiss cheese can be purchased only in Switzerland. Of those which are available to non-natives, the best known is Emmenthaler. This is the cheese most people have in mind when they think of "Swiss cheese"—it's the one with all the holes. Gruyere, another popular export, also has holes, but they're smaller and the cheese itself is more flavorful than Emmenthaler.

There's a very sound reason why a genuine Gruyere or Emmenthaler tastes so rich. Loving care goes into making these cheeses, and they just can't be rushed through assembly line production. The first step in making the cheeses is to curdle milk. Curdling causes milk to separate into whey, a liquid part, and curd, a solid protein part. The separation is hastened by adding rennet, a natural coagulant. Cultures which are added to the curdled mixture ensure the correct development of proper flavor and texture. After the cheese culture has been well mixed into the curd and whey, a cloth bag is used to gather up the curd. (The porous cloth used is appropriately called "cheesecloth.") After the whey drains from the cloth, the bag containing the curd is placed into a cheese mold, where the remaining liquid is squeezed out and the cheese is formed into the shape of a giant wheel. After a day of constant pressure, the cheese wheel is released and left to rest in a warm room. Rows of wheels ferment quietly on grooved pieces of circular-shaped wood. Every few days, the cheese is turned over, washed, and salted; this helps to preserve it as it ages. At this stage, a rind forms and thickens on the surface. Natural gases from the cheese culture form inside the wheel and produce the trademark holes. After aging at least 180 days, the cheese is ready to be sliced.

Before mentioning my other favorite Swiss foods, one additional cheese deserves special attention. If you want to enjoy a time-honored Swiss appetizer, you must purchase a Raclette cheese at your local store. This cheese may well make you spurn any other after you taste it melted. The traditional way to serve raclette, you see, is to cut it and turn the cut side toward a blazing fire. If you don't have a fireplace, use any open flame or even a charcoal grill outside. Make sure to put the raclette on a nonflammable surface. As the cheese melts, scrape off the hot bubbly top layer, and transfer the melted cheese to individual heated plates. Serve raclette with a freshly boiled potato and some sweet pickles. In this combination the foods perfectly complement one another; you won't believe how easy it is to have an appetizer turn into a main course if you don't tell your company more food is on the way.

Like other countries where dairies abound, Switzerland has ample beef and veal available for the food market. Swiss specialties feature smoked and fresh meats. I especially like veal and I often favor emincé de veau, veal that is cut into thin strips and cooked in a cream and white wine sauce, or veal cordon bleu, sautéed veal scallops stuffed with cheese and ham. I also like Swiss steak, beef simmered with tomatoes and peppers in a Dutch oven, and I recommend that you serve Swiss style fried potatoes, called rosti, with any meat dish. Rosti potatoes are similar in appearance to American hash browns. They are shredded potatoes mixed with finely chopped onions that are sauteed in butter and vegetable oil, and which look like a big crispy pancake when done.

Chocolate lovers: when it's time for dessert, Switzerland is your heaven on earth. Nothing compares to a Swiss chocolate dessert fondue. Melted together with fresh nuts, this unbelievable concoction simmering in a fondue pot awaits dunkables of fresh fruits and cake. For a lighter sweet touch, try meringues filled with ice cream or chiffon cake with chocolate cream cheese icing. Serve wine with dinner, and, if you're sampling fondues in Switzerland, don't pass up a chance to taste the local white wines. The Swiss make some wonderful wines, but very few are exported. When the grapes are harvested, many people take vacations and spend their time picking the fruit. Professionals, including doctors and lawyers, find this a way to get out into the fresh air, and everyone enjoys participating. When the wine is made, most Swiss feel that it belongs at home for the enjoyment of those who worked so hard to make the production possible.

Enjoy coffee after your meal, and give all the kids some Swiss hot chocolate. Now take a deep breath . . . can't you smell the mountain air?

Classic Cheese Fondue

If you have a crock pot, you can use it to prepare the following recipe. Please try to use imported, natural Swiss cheeses in your fondue. It's aged much longer and the flavor is richer than other "swiss" cheeses. To add variety to this dish, put in small amounts of your choice of crisp bacon bits, caraway seeds, or Worcestershire sauce.

Dunkables:

Before starting to make the fondue, prepare bite-size dunkables from the following:

Ham	**Bread cubes (cut so that each**
Fresh apples	**cube has a crust on one**
Boiled shrimp	**side; use French bread)**

Prepare enough dunkables for four people.

The fondue:

1 clove garlic	2 tablespoons flour
2 cups Emmenthaler cheese, shredded	2 cups light dry white wine (a Chablis is good)
2 cups Gruyere cheese, or 1 cup Gruyere and 1 cup Fontina cheese, shredded	2 tablespoons kirsch
	Dash nutmeg
	Salt and white pepper

Note: If you choose to use the fontina cheese, the texture of the fondue will be creamier.

Rub the garlic clove on the inside of the fondue pot and discard the used clove. Shred the cheeses, and sprinkle the flour over them.

Toss to distribute the flour evenly. Heat the wine in a small sauce-pan. Watch carefully, and when heat bubbles first appear on the surface of the wine, begin adding the cheese a little at a time. (Be careful not to let the wine boil; start adding cheese as soon as the bubbles first appear.) Stir mixture constantly with a wooden spoon and continue adding all of the cheese. When the mixture is smooth and well-blended, add kirsch, nutmeg, salt and pepper to taste. (I recommend just a pinch of salt and about ¼ teaspoon of white pepper.) Pour the fondue into the fondue pot, and place the pot over the fondue warmer at your table. For a well-rounded meal, serve this fondue with a crisp green salad. Tradition calls for serving white wine as a beverage with a cheese fondue. *(Serves 4)*

Beef or Lamb Fondue

Cheese fondues are completely Swiss. The use of meat reflects a French influence, and the idea has become so popular that it's assumed to be a Swiss invention. When choosing a fondue set to use with meat, try to find one that has different markings on each handle so each person knows his own utensil. I like to put the different sauces on a lazy Susan server, for added convenience.

1½–2 pounds beef sirloin or tenderloin, or lamb	Vegetable oil

Cut meat into ¾″ cubes. Heat vegetable oil in a fondue pot; about one-third of the pot should be filled—more will cause spattering oil to escape from the pot when the meat is cooked. When the oil is hot, skewer individual pieces of meat on fondue forks and cook to taste. Ten to twenty seconds of cooking yields rare meat, and fifty seconds yields well-done meat. Serve with the following sauces for dipping. *(Serves 4)*

Barbecue Sauce for Fondue

2 tablespoons butter	1 tablespoon lemon juice
1 small onion	2 tablespoons honey
1 garlic clove	¼ teaspoon powdered mustard
½ cup minced mushrooms	1 teaspoon Worcestershire
8 oz. tomato sauce	sauce

Melt butter in a small skillet. While butter melts, peel and chop the onion. Sauté chopped onion and garlic in the butter until the onion is transparent. Add remaining ingredients and simmer for 30 minutes. Serve hot.

Curry Sauce for Fondue

1 cup sour cream	1 teaspoon minced fresh
1 teaspoon cumin	parsley (or ¼ teaspoon
	dried parsley)
	1 teaspoon lemon juice

Combine all of the above in a small bowl. Serve chilled.

Sweet and Sour Sauce for Fondue

½ cup plum preserves	¼ teaspoon powdered mustard
¼ cup dry red wine	

Combine the above in a small saucepan. Heat and serve.

Scallop Fondue

1½ pounds fresh scallops   Vegetable oil

Wash and dry scallops. Add oil to fondue pot (fill one-third full). When the oil is hot, skewer individual scallops with fondue forks and cook to taste. Serve with the following dipping sauces. *(Serves 4)*

Mayonnaise Seafood Fondue Sauce

1 cup mayonnaise   1 teaspoon horseradish
2 teaspoons lemon juice   2 tablespoons minced pickle
2 teaspoons minced scallion

Combine all of the above in a small bowl. Serve chilled.

Sour Cream Seafood Fondue Sauce

1 cup sour cream   2 teaspoons sugar
¼ cup minced cucumber, seeds   ¼ teaspoon crushed red chili
  removed   pepper (optional)
2 teaspoons red wine vinegar

Combine all of the above in a small bowl. Serve chilled.

Tomato Seafood Fondue Sauce

8 ounces tomato sauce   ¼ cup orange marmalade
¼ cup soy sauce   2 tablespoons fresh lemon juice

Combine all of the above and heat in a small saucepan. Serve hot.

Serve the above fondues with a crisp green salad or a fresh fruit salad and French bread.

Swiss Style Fried Potatoes

Swiss style fried (Rosti) potatoes may be served with any main course in this section. They are similar to American hash browns, and I like them for breakfast as well as for meals served later in the day. Experiment with the flavor of these potatoes by adding small bits of chopped green pepper, crisp cooked bacon, chopped mushrooms, or tomatoes and cheese. They should be served on a heated plate so that they stay nice and warm.

8 medium white potatoes	8 tablespoons vegetable oil
½ teaspoon salt	8 tablespoons sweet butter
1 medium onion	Salt and pepper

Peel potatoes and cut them in half. Place potatoes in a large saucepan and cover with water, adding ½ teaspoon salt. Bring to a boil and reduce heat so that potatoes continue to boil slowly. Cook potatoes about 12 minutes, so that they are not cooked all the way through. Drain water from the parboiled potatoes, and allow them to cool. Cover the potatoes and refrigerate for several hours.

When ready to prepare, first peel and chop the onion into fine pieces. Shred the cold potatoes into long, thin strips using a food processor or a stand-up grater and shredding the potatoes on the side of the grater with the largest holes. Heat 4 tablespoons vegetable oil and 4 tablespoons sweet butter in a large skillet (preferably cast iron) and, while the butter and oil heat, toss the onion with the shredded potatoes. When the melted butter and oil combination is very hot, evenly distribute the onions and potatoes in the skillet. Fry over moderate heat until the potatoes are well-browned on the bottom. Loosen the potato cake with a metal spatula, and slide the cake out of the pan onto a large plate, being careful not to break or split the cake. Add the remaining butter and oil to the skillet. Lightly butter a second large plate, and place it over the plate holding the potatoes. Invert the two plates so that the uncooked side of the potato cake rests on the buttered plate. Slide the cake back into the skillet, and brown the second side. Cook about 12–15 minutes. Season to taste with salt and pepper. *(Serves 4–6)*

Creamy Salad Dressing

Make this dressing ahead of time; it's cooked on top of the stove, and chilled before serving. It goes perfectly with salad that follows.

2 tablespoons flour	2 eggs
½ teaspoon salt	1 cup light cream
½ teaspoon dry mustard	4 tablespoons fresh lemon juice
1 tablespoon sugar	

Mix flour, salt, dry mustard, and sugar together in a small bowl. Lightly beat eggs in a second bowl; combine eggs and flour mixture, using a whisk to blend. Add light cream and continue blending until all ingredients are mixed thoroughly. Pour dressing into the top of a double boiler. Gradually bring the water in the bottom of the double boiler to a boil, and then reduce heat so that water simmers. Be sure to whisk the dressing constantly during this process, so that lumps do not form as the dressing thickens. When the dressing has thickened (about 5 minutes of cooking), remove from heat and whisk in lemon juice. Chill well and toss with Swiss salad. *(Makes approximately 1½ cups of dressing)*

Swiss Salad

This very simple salad becomes a gourmet delight when served in combination with Creamy Salad Dressing.

1 small white cabbage (large enough to make 3 cups shredded cabbage)	2 tart apples ¼ fresh lemon ½ pound natural Swiss cheese

Shred the cabbage; measure three cups into a large bowl. Peel, core, and slice apples into thin bite-size pieces; sprinkle apple slices with lemon and add to cabbage. Shred the cheese and add it to the cabbage and apples. Pour on the creamy salad dressing, and toss so that dressing is evenly distributed. *(Serves 4)*

Veal Baked with Sour Cream

This recipe for veal chops is easy and convenient and also worthy of serving on special occasions. Each chop has an individual smothering of sour cream that adds a special flavor treat to each bite.

2 tablespoons butter	⅛ teaspoon pepper
4 lean veal chops	4 slices sweet onion
1 tablespoon chopped fresh parsley (or ¼ teaspoon dried parsley)	½ cup chicken stock
	1 cup sour cream
¼ teaspoon salt	⅓ cup grated Gruyere cheese

Preheat oven to 350° F. Melt butter in a large skillet. Sauté chops in butter until each side is light brown. Arrange browned chops in a single layer in a large baking dish. Sprinkle with parsley, salt, and pepper. Separate onion slices into rings, and arrange the rings over the top of the veal. Mix the chicken stock with the pan drippings from the skillet, and pour the liquid over the onions and veal. Bake covered for 45 minutes. Remove from oven after 45 minutes, and cover top of meat with sour cream. Sprinkle the Gruyere cheese on top of the cream. Bake 15–20 minutes uncovered, or until cheese has melted and is golden brown. *(Serves 4)*

Veal Cordon Bleu

4 veal scallops, about 6″ x 4″	¼ pound imported Swiss cheese
½ fresh lemon	4 slices boiled ham
2 eggs	½ cup vegetable oil
½ cup flour	Salt and pepper
1 cup bread crumbs	Fresh watercress

Pound veal scallops until they're about ⅛″ thick (no thicker than ¼″). Sprinkle veal with fresh lemon juice from the ½ lemon. Set meat aside. Lightly beat the eggs in a medium-size bowl. Put flour into another bowl, and bread crumbs into a third bowl. Slice the cheese into four equal strips. Dip each veal scallop first in egg, and then cover each scallop evenly with flour. Wrap each piece of cheese in a slice of ham. Place ham and cheese in the center of the scallops; fold veal in half over the ham and cheese, and dip the resulting cutlet in egg once more. Dip folded scallop in bread crumbs, covering all sides thoroughly. Refrigerate veal for two hours. When ready to cook, heat vegetable oil in a large skillet. Fry stuffed veal until golden brown and crisp on both sides. Season to taste with salt and pepper. Garnish with fresh watercress. *(Serves 4)*

Emincé de Veau

This recipe for veal in cream sauce is my favorite way to enjoy veal.

1½ pounds veal scallops
 1 tablespoon flour
 2 tablespoons vegetable oil
1½ tablespoons flour plus
     3 tablespoons water
 2 tablespoons butter

2 tablespoons scallion (mainly
     white part) sliced thinly
½ cup dry white wine
1 cup heavy cream
Salt and pepper

Cut veal into thin strips about ½" thick. Sprinkle veal evenly with 1 tablespoon flour and set aside. Heat vegetable oil in large skillet. Brown floured veal lightly in oil; remove and set aside. Combine 1½ tablespoons flour with 3 tablespoons water to make a smooth paste. Set the paste aside. Melt butter in the same skillet used to sauté the veal. Sauté the scallion in the butter, then add the wine, and boil for one minute. Reduce the heat and add half of the cream to the skillet. When this mixture begins to simmer, add 2 tablespoons of the remaining cream to the flour and water paste, then add mixture to the pan, stirring rapidly and continuously to thicken the sauce. Add the remaining cream and stir. Add the cooked veal, and simmer until meat is warmed through. Season to taste with salt and pepper. *(Serves 4)*

Swiss Steak

1½ pounds round steak, cut into
 four pieces
2 tablespoons flour
¼ teaspoon salt
⅛ teaspoon black pepper
3 tablespoons vegetable oil

1 green pepper
2 fresh tomatoes
1 medium onion
2 tablespoons tomato paste
2 cups beef stock
1 cup fresh mushrooms

Sprinkle steak with flour, salt, and pepper. Heat the vegetable oil in a Dutch oven. Add steak to the hot oil, and brown well on both sides. While steak browns, remove seeds from green pepper and slice into thin rings. Slice tomatoes, and peel and slice onion. Mix tomato paste with beef stock. Add liquid to the Dutch oven, and add pepper, tomatoes, and onion. Reduce heat and simmer steak for 1½–2 hours, or until meat is very tender. Cut mushrooms in half, add to steak, and simmer an additional five minutes. *(Serves 4)*

Swiss Cinnamon Chicken

This elegant, simple dish is quite impressive in appearance and is perfect to serve at a dinner party.

4 large chicken breast fillets
1 large bunch broccoli
2 tablespoons butter
1 large slice of sweet onion
¾–1 cup dry red wine (depending on size of filets)

¼ teaspoon cinnamon
Salt and pepper
4–6 large slices Emmenthaler cheese

Wash and dry chicken breasts; set aside. Wash and trim broccoli. Cut broccoli into spears and steam until almost tender. Remove from heat and set aside. In a large Dutch oven, melt the butter. Chop the onion into small pieces and sauté in butter until transparent. Add chicken to Dutch oven and brown lightly on both sides. Add wine, cinnamon, and a dash of salt and pepper. Cover Dutch oven, reduce heat, and simmer for one hour, turning chicken over once after 30 minutes. At the end of one hour, cover chicken pieces with steamed broccoli and top broccoli with cheese. Cover and simmer several minutes until cheese melts. Serve with rice and mushrooms, made according to the following recipe. *(Serves 4)*

Brown Rice with Mushrooms

This rice dish goes exceptionally well with Swiss cinnamon chicken. I'm sure you'll like it with many other foods, too.

Brown rice:

1 cup brown rice	2 tablespoons butter
2½ cups water	½ teaspoon salt

Put all the ingredients into a saucepan with a tightly fitting lid. Bring to a boil, reduce heat, and then simmer, covered, for 45 minutes. Remove from heat and set aside.

Mushrooms:

5 tablespoons butter	Salt and pepper
1 cup chopped onion	¼ cup dry red wine
3 cups sliced fresh mushrooms	

Melt butter in a large skillet. Add onion to melted butter and saute until transparent. Add sliced mushrooms, dash of salt and pepper, and wine. Simmer uncovered for 30 minutes, until liquid is greatly reduced. Add cooked brown rice, stir well, and serve. *(Serves 4)*

Broiled Calves Liver

The following is an elaborate way of preparing this dish. For a quicker, simpler variation, slice onions (use one very large one, if you like) and sauté it with several slices of bacon. When the bacon and onion have cooked, set them aside and sauté the liver (you don't have to cut it into pieces) in the bacon fat. Serve buttered spinach as a side dish and arrange cooked bacon and onions over liver.

Calves Liver on Skewers

Liver with bacon, onion, and fresh spinach is a delightful, colorful, and nutritious combination.

1½ pounds fresh spinach	16 slices bacon
1 garlic clove	1 tablespoon vegetable oil
24 small white onions	8 skewers
1½ pounds calves liver	2 tablespoons butter
Salt, pepper	

Wash spinach well. Place garlic clove into small amount of water in bottom of vegetable steamer; steam spinach and, when it's cooked, remove steamer from heat and set aside. Peel and steam onions until almost cooked through. Remove onions from heat and set aside. Cut liver into 32 cubes and sprinkle with salt and pepper. Preheat broiler. Cut bacon slices in half. Wrap each liver cube in ½ bacon slice. Rub a small amount of vegetable oil on each skewer; put bacon-wrapped liver on skewers (4 liver cubes and 3 onions on each), and broil on all sides until bacon is crisp. Add butter to cooked spinach; heat gently in vegetable steamer until butter melts. Arrange spinach on serving platter, place liver on spinach, and serve. *(Serves 4)*

Cheese/Wheat Bread

This bread turns a ham sandwich into a gourmet treat. I enjoy ham sandwiches with cream cheese on this bread, grilled, for a special surprise combination.

4 cups whole wheat flour	⅔ cup vegetable oil
1½ cups white flour	½ cup brown sugar
2 tablespoons baking powder	4 tablespoons finely minced
1½ teaspoons salt	onion
2 teaspoons baking soda	2 cups shredded Swiss cheese
4 eggs	(imported preferred)
3 cups milk	

Preheat oven to 375° F. Butter and flour two loaf pans; set aside. Sift together flours, baking powder, salt, and baking soda, and put into a large bowl. In a second bowl, beat together eggs and milk. Add vegetable oil, brown sugar, and onion to egg mixture. Gradually stir liquid into flour. Stir well and add shredded cheese, mixing until cheese is blended into the batter. Pour into pans and bake for 50–55 minutes. Cool bread slightly and remove from pans. After bread has cooled completely, store well-wrapped in refrigerator. *(Makes 2 loaves)*

Swiss Meringues

These meringues are soft and shiny; sugar is folded into the meringue, and the finished baked product sparkles in the light.

6 egg whites	**½ teaspoon almond extract**
1½ teaspoons cream of tartar	**¼ teaspoon salt**
½ teaspoon vanilla extract	**1¼ cups sugar**

Preheat the oven to 250° F. Combine egg whites, cream of tartar, vanilla, almond flavoring, and salt. Beat mixture to soft peaks. Gradually add 1 cup of the sugar to the egg whites while continuing to beat until stiff peaks are formed. Fold in remaining sugar to give the meringue a shiny gloss after it bakes. Butter a cookie sheet, and form 3" ovals of meringue on the cookie sheet using a tablespoon to shape individual meringues *or* put the meringue into a pastry bag and squeeze the ovals directly onto the cookie sheet. Bake 25–30 minutes. Cool and fill meringues with choice of ice cream, fruit, or custard when ready to serve. *(Serves 6)*

Chiffon Cake

Chiffon cake is baked in a tube pan. After you take the cake from the oven, invert it until the cake has cooled. Then loosen from pan by running a thin knife around the outer edge and the center. I sometimes find it helpful to tap the pan against a countertop to further loosen the cake. It should then come out easily. When serving, use a knife with a serrated cutting edge so that the cake is not compressed when it is sliced.

1¾ cups flour	½ cup vegetable oil
3 teaspoons baking powder	½ teaspoon rum extract
½ teaspoon salt	1 teaspoon vanilla extract
1 teaspoon cinnamon	7 egg whites
½ teaspoon nutmeg	¾ cup water
1½ cups sugar	1 tablespoon confectioner's
¼ cup ground walnuts	sugar (optional)
7 egg yolks	

Preheat oven to 325° F. Sift together flour, baking powder, salt, cinnamon, and nutmeg. Put sifted ingredients into a large bowl. Add sugar and walnuts and mix well. Lightly beat egg yolks in a separate bowl. Add oil and both extracts to the beaten eggs. In another bowl, beat egg whites until stiff. Set aside. Alternately add egg yolks and water to dry ingredients. Mix well and then gently fold the beaten egg whites into the batter. Gently pour the batter into an ungreased tube pan. Bake for 60–70 minutes, or until a toothpick inserted into the center of the cake comes out clean. Remove from pan as directed above and cool. If desired, sprinkle the top with confectioner's sugar.

Surprise Crescents

The surprise is the preserves with which these rich cookies are filled. These cookies are made with just four ingredients, and they're incredibly delicious.

6 ounces cream cheese	**2 cups sifted flour**
½ pound melted butter	**Your choice of preserves**

Soften cream cheese at room temperature. In a large bowl, combine cream cheese and melted butter. Gradually add flour to make a smooth dough. Form the dough into a ball, and chill for several hours. Preheat oven to 425° F. Divide dough into two parts. Roll out the dough until it's no more than ⅛″ thick. Cut out circles of dough using a 3″ cookie cutter. Put a teaspoon of your favorite preserves on each dough circle. Fold circle over and pinch edges closed so preserves stay inside. For a rich brown color, brush top of crescent with a mixture of beaten egg mixed with a tablespoon of milk. Bake for 12 minutes, until top of cookie is golden brown, on an ungreased cookie sheet. *(Makes about 45 cookies)*

Chocolate Cream Cheese Icing

This rich icing goes well with the chiffon cake or on any cake of your choice. The addition of cream cheese makes the icing less sweet and also makes it extremely smooth. If you prefer a thinner icing, add more cream. For a very thick, fudgelike icing, use less cream.

4 tablespoons sweet butter	2½ cups confectioner's sugar
1 square unsweetened Swiss Baker's chocolate	½ teaspoon vanilla extract
3 ounces cream cheese	2 tablespoons light cream

Melt sweet butter and chocolate together in the top of a double boiler. Add cream cheese to pot, and stir until cream cheese has softened. Pour mixture into a bowl, stir in sugar, and mix well. Add vanilla extract and cream.

Chocolate Dessert Fondue

I love surprising friends with unusual dunkables served with a dessert fondue. Any type of fresh fruit is perfect with this after dinner dish. Try melon, bananas, strawberries, pineapple, cherries —whatever your favorite is. Also serve any firm cake you like; the chiffon cake in this section is a very good selection, as is pound cake.

> 2 squares Swiss Baker's
>   unsweetened chocolate
> 4 ounces sweet milk chocolate
> ¾ cup light cream
>
> 3 tablespoons kirsch
> 3 tablespoons sugar
> ¼ cup slivered almonds
>   (optional)

Melt chocolate in the top of a double boiler. Add cream and kirsch, stir well, and gradually add sugar, stirring until the sugar is completely dissolved. Add almonds, if you wish. Pour mixture into fondue pot. *(Serves 6)*

Chinese Cuisine

Introduction

We all have "sentimental food favorites" that we love because of the meaning they hold for us. These foods are synonymous with a special place, a special person, or a special time in our lives. Some things will never be the same after the first time we experience them—we can recapture the memory but never again the moment. Sometimes, however, the memory enriches the moment. So it is when we reminisce about our youth. Think of being home and sitting down to Sunday dinner when you were a child. Go through the list of all the good things you had to eat and suddenly there you are, just about to sink your teeth into Mom's best dish. And whatever your personal favorite, from a pot roast or Thanksgiving turkey, to chicken soup or chocolate cake, all you need is the thought of that dish, the slightest hint of that same aroma, and you're home again.

For me, the food that recalls my childhood is chiao tze, Northern Chinese dumplings stuffed with meat and vegetables. They look almost like ravioli, and for me they were an extra special treat because our family chef would make them just for me every

Sunday. Chiao tze is also a very versatile dish. Men would take the dumplings with them on hunting and camping trips so that they wouldn't have to carry anything else for food until they captured some game. They'd fill a kettle with snow, and set it over the campfire to melt. When the water from the snow started to boil, they'd add the dumplings, and after the chiao tze were cooked, they'd also have a broth to drink.

Chiao tze were also a source of inadvertent amusement. At that time in Northern China, modern refrigeration was a thing of the future. But that didn't trouble the local chefs, who developed an ingenious way of freezing a few weeks' supply of dumplings at a time: It was so cold outside that they used to just throw the chiao tze out of the kitchen window into the snow piled up next to the house. You could be walking down the street and suddenly see a bunch of dumplings go flying through the air to land in a snow drift. The best part of all this was that, whenever you wanted a quick meal, all you had to do was walk outside, gather up some chiao tze, take them back into the kitchen, and cook them.

Chiao tze is a perfect example of the seemingly endless assortment of unique Chinese foods. China is roughly the same size as the United States, and like any large country, the national fare is extremely varied. There are four major types of cuisine. Divided into region, they are Mandarin (north), Cantonese (south), Shanghai (east), and Szechuan (west). While there's an inevitable blending of foods from all four areas, certain specialties can be singled out. Fish made with sweet and sour sauce is a Mandarin dish; steamed fish is Cantonese. Shanghai chefs are known for noodle specialties, and Szechuan cooking features hot, spicy foods. Whatever the dish, it's always served with rice or noodles. Meats, poultry, and seafood, combined with vegetables, are really served as complementary side dishes to the all-important grains. Since meat is quite expensive in China, this practice allows a little bit to go a long way, and also lets the cook present a choice of different flavors at each meal.

Ideally, a Chinese chef blends foods of contrasting color, texture, and flavor in each individual side dish. He uses at least two opposing textures, choosing from soft, crisp, smooth, tender, and crunchy foods. Contrast follows contrast: a cold dish after a hot one, rich and spicy foods after bland foods, sweet dishes after salty dishes. Colors vary and yet look pleasing together. For an illustration of the execution of these culinary principles, let's consider sweet and sour sea bass. The fish is fried so that the outside is crispy, but the inside remains tender. The sauce served as an accompaniment contains both sugar and vinegar and is thus simultaneously sweet and sour. The sea bass is rich golden brown outside, pure white inside, and is further complemented by soft, bright yellow pineapple and crisp, green snow pea pods. The final result is a dish that pleases all of your senses as well as your appetite.

For several reasons, Chinese meals take a short time to cook. First of all, much of the cooking is done by stir-frying in a wok, a large pan with deep, gently sloping sides that distributes heat more evenly than a conventional pan. (If you don't have a wok, use a deep-sided, heavy, frying pan.) The second reason is that meats, poultry, and vegetables are usually cut into bite-size pieces before cooking. Third, all ingredients are prepared in advance so that the cooking process itself is a series of smooth, easy steps. When you're going to stir-fry, first slice, dice, shred, or mince each ingredient as called for in the recipe. The ideal utensil to use for this is a Chinese cleaver. Note that recipes for stir-fried foods often call for marinating meat, fish, or poultry in various sauces. If you cut the meat and set it aside to marinate first, it will be ready for the pan after you finish preparing the other ingredients. If you cut meat against the grain, by the way, it will be more tender after it's cooked. Also, partially frozen meat is much easier to slice into thin pieces. Cut firm vegetables such as carrots or celery on a diagonal to increase their cooking surfaces. Cut tender vegetables such as mushrooms or scallions straight through. Keep each ingredient in a separate bowl, or at least in separate piles on your chopping board, since each item is added to the wok according to the length of time it needs to cook.

Stir-frying is a marvelous way to cook. It saves time, preserves more of foods' natural vitamins and minerals, and uses less fuel. The high heat that cooks food so quickly also causes the release of its natural juices. The blending of these liquids with marinades always gives you delicious sauces. Stir-frying isn't at all like deep-fat frying. With a wok, you only need a small amount of oil, enough to just coat the food. Let the oil get very hot before you start cooking. (Woks, incidentally, are also used for steaming and stewing.)

The basic sauces and spices needed for Chinese cooking are easy to find. Besides soy sauce, you'll need dry sherry, sugar, ginger, vinegar, garlic, salt and hot chili peppers. More exotic ingredients such as fermented (salted) black beans or hoisin sauce can be purchased in local specialty shops or by mail-order. All specialty stores also stock inventories of different types of soy sauces. Cook daringly and try them all.

Set a traditional Chinese table to show off your good cooking. Include a tea cup, pair of chopsticks, medium-size plate, one bowl that doubles for both soup and rice, porcelain soup spoon, and small saucer for soy sauce for each guest. Serve the food family style, with all dishes placed in the center of the table. Make as many different dishes as you want—variety is part of the fun of Chinese dining. On a recent visit to Hong Kong, I attended a dinner featuring specialties from more than a dozen restaurants. Each dish represented a different local cooking style. You can indulge in the same kind of treat for your family and friends by serving an assortment of appetizers, soup, rice, and main dishes, some of which may be made in advance.

End your Chinese banquet with cookies and fresh fruits. Serve tea before and after eating, and be prepared to hear endless compliments.

Chiao Tze

When you make my favorite dumplings, first prepare the filling and then make the dough. For the seafood filling, it is important that you use fresh, not frozen, seafood.

Pork with Vegetables Filling

1 pound lean ground pork
¼ cup finely chopped water
    chestnuts
¼ cup finely chopped fresh
    mushrooms
¼ cup finely chopped bamboo
    shoots
2 tablespoons finely minced
    scallion

2 slices fresh ginger (about 1"
    across), finely minced, or ¼
    teaspoon powdered ginger
½ teaspoon salt
2 tablespoons soy sauce
2 tablespoons chicken stock
1 tablespoon cornstarch
1 egg

Although the Chinese do not traditionally do so, I sometimes sauté the pork in a skillet, to ensure it is well done, and drain off the fat. While the pork cooks, prepare the chopped and minced vegetables. (A food processor helps.) Combine the cooked pork with all the vegetables in a large bowl. Mix well and then add ginger, salt, soya, and chicken stock. Mix again and then add the cornstarch and the egg. Stir a final time and set aside. *(Makes filling for 35–40 dumplings)*

Crab with Chinese Cabbage Filling

1 cup finely chopped Chinese
   cabbage
½ teaspoon salt
10 ounces lightly cooked minced
   crab meat (or shrimp)
2 tablespoons finely minced
   scallion

2 tablespoons chicken stock
1 tablespoon soy sauce
1 tablespoon dry sherry
1 teaspoon sugar
1 envelope unflavored gelatin

Put the chopped cabbage into a small bowl with a wide opening. Sprinkle the salt over the cabbage and place a weighted cover on top of the cabbage. Let stand for 20 minutes and then place cabbage inside a cheesecloth. Squeeze well to remove excess liquid. (This is a very important step; if the liquid is not removed, the filling will be too moist.) Put the cabbage into a large bowl, and add the crab, scallion, stock, soy, sherry, and sugar. Stir to mix thoroughly, and then add the gelatin. Stir again and set aside. *(Makes filling for 35–40 dumplings)*

Dough:

2 cups plus 2 tablespoons flour
1 cup boiling water

1 teaspoon sesame oil

Put flour into a large bowl and make a small well in the center of the flour. Combine boiling water with sesame oil, and gradually add the liquid to the flour. Stir the mixture constantly with a wooden fork or chopsticks until a crumbly dough forms. Wait a few minutes for the dough to cool, and then knead the dough until it's smooth and soft. If necessary, add a small amount of extra flour to keep the dough from sticking to the sides of the bowl. Form a single round ball of dough, and then cover the bowl. Set aside and let stand 15 minutes.

Dumplings:

Divide the dough in half. Shape each half into a ball. Put one dough ball back into the bowl and cover. Roll out the other ball into a circle no thicker than ⅛". Using a round cookie cutter with a 3" diameter, cut out circles of dough. Combine excess dough with remaining dough ball; roll dough out into a second circle and continue cutting out 3" circles. Continue until all dough is used up. *(Makes 35–40 circles)*

Place 1–2 teaspoons of filling in the center of each circle. Fold the dough over to form a half-circle, and pinch edges together, forming filled crescents. If dough does not seal easily, moisten edges slightly. Steam the dumplings for 20 minutes on a rack over boiling water. If you like, you may fry the dumplings after they are steamed. Serve with the following sauce for dipping.

Dipping Sauce

½ cup chicken broth
1–2 tablespoons soy sauce
2 teaspoons vinegar
1 teaspoon sugar
1 teaspoon dry sherry

1 tablespoon minced scallion
Hot chili oil (optional)
Flaked red chili pepper
(optional)

Combine broth, soy, vinegar, sugar, and sherry. Garnish with scallion. Experiment with making a more robust sauce by adding hot chili oil or flaked red chili pepper to taste.

Lotus Blossom Spare Ribs

Hoisin sauce has a rich, aromatic flavor and gives this dish its special taste. You can order hoisin sauce from Chinese mail-order supply stores or find it in your local Chinese market. If you're unable to purchase hoisin sauce, try using a commercial smoke-flavored barbeque sauce. The flavor won't be quite the same, but the resulting ribs are very good.

16–20 large individual pork spare ribs	4 tablespoons dry sherry
2 tablespoons hoisin sauce	1 tablespoon honey
4 tablespoons soy sauce	1 tablespoon light brown sugar
3 cloves garlic	2 tablespoons vinegar

Separate ribs. Combine hoisin, soy, garlic, sherry, honey, sugar, and vinegar. Pour sauce over ribs in a large, shallow container and marinate for 30 minutes. Preheat broiler. Broil ribs 12–15 minutes on each side, basting frequently with marinade. When ribs are cooked through and covered with a rich, almost carmelized coating, serve at once. If desired, you can heat remaining marinade to serve in a separate bowl as additional dipping sauce. (*Serves 4 as appetizer*)

Stuffed Mushrooms

1 pound large mushrooms
½ pound ground pork
¼ cup minced water chestnuts
¼ cup minced scallion
2 teaspoons cornstarch
2 slices ginger (about 1″ across), minced

½ teaspoon hot chili oil
1 beaten egg
2 teaspoons soy sauce
¼ cup vegetable oil
1 tablespoon sesame seeds

Preheat oven to 350° F. Remove stems from mushrooms; chop stems and combine with pork, minced water chestnuts, and minced scallion. Mix in egg and soy sauce. Stuff mushroom caps with pork and vegetable mixture. Dip bottom of mushrooms into vegetable oil to coat generously, and place into a large, shallow baking dish in a single layer. Sprinkle with sesame seeds, and bake for 30–35 minutes. Serve with extra soy sauce on the side. (*Serves 4 as appetizer*)

Ginger Soy Beef

The proportions in the recipe for ginger soy beef are for an appetizer to serve four. To serve as a main dish, double the ingredients and add additional water so that there is a natural gravy.

1 pound chuck steak	2 teaspoons cornstarch
3 scallions	1 tablespoon dry sherry
3 tablespoons vegetable oil	1 tablespoon brown sugar
2 slices ginger (about 1"	4 tablespoons soy sauce
across), minced, or ¼	1 cup hot water
teaspoon powdered ginger	

Use a cleaver to cut the beef into bite-size cubes. Cut scallions into 1" pieces. Heat oil in wok or heavy skillet. Add scallions and ginger to oil, stir, and add beef. Brown beef on all sides. While beef cooks, mix cornstarch with sherry, brown sugar, and soy sauce. Add to meat, cook for several minutes, and then add hot water. Bring liquid to boil, reduce heat, and simmer uncovered for 25 minutes. To serve, skewer meat with toothpicks, if using as an appetizer, and serve hot sauce on the side. If using as a main dish, serve meat and sauce together in a large serving bowl. (*Serves 4 as appetizer*)

Cold Asparagus Salad

This simple salad is refreshing and easy to make.

20 stalks fresh asparagus
2 tablespoons soy sauce
2 teaspoons vegetable oil

2 teaspoons sugar
1 teaspoon sesame seeds

Break off asparagus stems a few inches from the bottom. As you bend the spear, you'll see where the vegetable naturally begins to break. This is the point where you should snap off the lower part of each stem. Steam asparagus until tender; set aside to cool. Mix soy, vegetable oil, and sugar together. Pour over cooled asparagus, and marinate one hour, turning vegetables after 30 minutes. Just before serving, drain off marinade and sprinkle asparagus with sesame seeds. *(Serves 4)*

Corn and Crab Soup

Although I include a recipe for making chicken stock so that you may prepare this soup completely from scratch, you can use commercially prepared chicken broth if you wish. The smooth texture of this soup combined with its subtle flavor make it a culinary delight.

Chicken Stock:

Giblets from one large
    chicken, plus wings and
    legs
5 cups water
1 large carrot
1 cup Chinese cabbage, cut into
    large pieces

2 scallions
1 tablespoon pickling spices
1 slice fresh ginger (about 1"
    across), cut into thin slivers,
    or ⅛ teaspoon powdered
    ginger

Wash giblets and chicken parts; set aside. Put water into medium-size soup pot. Cut carrot into several pieces; cut scallions into quarters. Add all vegetables and chicken to soup pot. Add pickling spices and ginger. Bring to boil, reduce heat, and simmer until liquid is reduced to three cups. Remove any foam that rises to the surface. Remove vegetables and chicken and then strain the stock.

Soup:

3 cups chicken stock	¾ cup fresh crab meat, cooked
1 cup cream-style corn	2 egg whites, beaten until
½ teaspoon salt	slightly frothy
1 slice ginger, minced	Dash white pepper
1 tablespoon cornstarch	1 tablespoon minced scallion
2 tablespoons water	

Bring stock to boil in a medium-size saucepan. Add cream-style corn and immediately reduce heat so that soup is barely simmering. Add salt and ginger; stir. In small bowl, combine cornstarch and water to make a smooth paste. Add a small amount of the soup to the paste, and then add the mixture to the soup, stirring constantly as you do so. Simmer gently another few minutes, as you stir the soup. Add crab, and stir until crab is heated. Add the beaten egg whites all at once to the soup, stir only once, and remove from heat. Garnish with dash of pepper and scallion. *(Serves 4)*

Vegetable Duck Soup

This is a very mild, healthful soup.

Duck Stock:

1 4–5 pound duck, with giblets
7 cups water
2 slices fresh ginger (about 1"
    across), cut into thin slices,
    or ¼ teaspoon powdered
    ginger

2 cloves garlic
2 carrots, sliced thinly

Wash duck and giblets; place them into a large soup pot. Add remaining ingredients and bring to boil. Reduce heat and simmer for several hours, skimming off foam that rises to the top of the broth. When liquid is reduced to about 4–5 cups (about two hours), cool broth. Skim off excess fat, remove duck, giblets, and vegetables, and strain the stock. When the duck is cool enough to handle, remove and shred the meat for use in the soup.

Soup:

4–5 cups duck stock
    Shredded duck meat from
    duck used in stock
1 cup sliced bamboo shoots
2 large scallions, cut into 1"
    slices

2 cups shredded Chinese
    cabbage
1 cup bean curd, cut into bite-
    size pieces

Bring duck stock to boil in a medium-size soup pot. Reduce heat so that stock simmers; add remaining ingredients in order, simmering for 10 minutes and stirring occasionally. Serve after 10 minutes; season to taste with salt or soy sauce and black pepper. *(Serves 4)*

Chinese Pickled Turnips

These vegetables have a piquant sweet-sour taste when cooked in the following manner. Pickled turnips complement almost any dish.

4 small white turnips	½ cup sugar
1½ teaspoons salt	2 heaping tablespoons honey
¾ cup white vinegar	¼ teaspoon yellow food color
¼ cup water	(optional)

Peel and slice turnips into thin slices. Sprinkle with salt and let stand one hour. Drain liquid from turnips after one hour, and place into small saucepan. Combine vinegar, water, sugar, honey, and optional yellow food color; pour over turnips. Bring to boil, turn down heat, and simmer partially covered until turnips are tender—about 40 minutes. Serve hot. *(Serves 4)*

Sautéed Broccoli

1 bunch of broccoli
4 tablespoons soy sauce
2 tablespoons dry sherry
1 teaspoon sugar
1 fresh red chili pepper, or
    dried chili pepper to taste
3 tablespoons vegetable oil

1 clove garlic
1 slice fresh ginger (about 1"
    across), minced, or ⅛
    teaspoon powdered ginger
½ cup cooked shredded roast
    pork (optional)

Separate broccoli into spears; trim off bottom of spears. Steam broccoli until spears are almost cooked but are still firm. Set aside. Mix together soy, sherry, and sugar. Cut chili pepper into thin slices and add to liquid; set aside. Heat oil in wok or heavy skillet. Saute garlic and ginger for one minute, add broccoli spears, and stir one minute. Pour sauce over broccoli and stir one minute. If you wish, garnish with roast pork. *(Serves 4)*

Rice

Choose a medium grain white variety if you purchase your rice from an Oriental market. When you are ready to cook, first rinse the rice in cold water until the water runs clear. (If you are using rice purchased in a regular supermarket, it will most likely be converted rice, and you do not need to rinse it.) Allow ¼ cup of uncooked rice per serving, and for each cup of uncooked rice, use 1¾ cup cold water for cooking. (For more moist rice, add a bit more water; for drier rice, use a bit less, according to taste preference.) Put rice and water together into a heavy pot that has a tightly fitting cover. Bring water and rice to a boil, then cover the pot and turn heat very low. Cook 20 minutes without stirring, and then remove from heat. Let stand 5–10 minutes, then fluff rice with chopsticks and serve.

Fried Rice

Use rice that you've made a day ahead or early in the same day to prepare fried rice.

2 eggs
½ cup vegetable oil
½ cup minced scallion
1 cup sliced water chestnuts
1 cup sliced mushrooms

1½ cups cubed roast pork OR 1½ cups cooked small shrimp
4 cups cooked rice
3 tablespoons soy sauce

Beat eggs lightly. Heat 1 tablespoon of the oil in a large skillet and add beaten eggs. Cook the eggs like a thin pancake. Remove egg, cool, and shred into thin strips. Set aside. Heat remaining oil in skillet, and add scallion, water chestnuts, mushrooms, and pork or shrimp. Stir for one minute and add cooked rice. Stir to blend ingredients, and sprinkle soy sauce over rice. Stir until soy is well-mixed into the rice and the rice is heated through—this will take only a few minutes. Add the shredded egg, stir once, and serve. *(Serves 6)*

New Year Fried Rice

In this dish, salt is used instead of soy sauce so that the rice remains white and forms a background for colorful bits of pork, pea pods, shrimp, chicken, sprouts, and egg.

2 eggs	½ cup snow pea pods
½ cup vegetable oil	4 cups cooked rice
½ cup diced roast pork	½ teaspoon salt
½ cup small cooked shrimp	1 cup pea sprouts
½ cup diced cooked chicken	

Beat eggs lightly. Heat 1 tablespoon of the oil in a large skillet. Add the beaten eggs and cook them like a thin pancake. Remove cooked eggs, cool, and shred into strips. Set aside. Heat remaining oil in skillet. Add pork, shrimp, chicken, and pea pods. Stir for one minute and add rice, stirring to heat rice through. Sprinkle salt over rice, stir, and add sprouts. Stir once more, add shredded egg, and serve. *(Serves 6)*

Mushroom Egg Foo Yung

This is a wonderfully versatile dish. If you have small amounts of meat, fish, or vegetables left over from other meals, you can make your own original versions of foo yung.

8 eggs	1 slice of fresh ginger (about 1″
1 cup sliced mushrooms	across), minced, or ⅛
½ cup thinly chopped onion	teaspoon powdered ginger
½ cup sliced water chestnuts	1 cup vegetable oil

Lightly beat eggs. Prepare vegetables and add them with the ginger to the eggs. Stir well and set aside. Heat 2 tablespoons of the oil in a small skillet; add ⅛ of egg and vegetable mixture to the skillet, and cook like a pancake. (There should be enough for 8 omelettes; use 2 tablespoons of oil per pancake.) Turn over each egg pancake once, when the bottom is lightly browned. As each one is cooked, keep it warm in a very low oven while you cook the rest. You may want to use two small skillets at once to speed up the process. Serve with the following gravy. *(Serves 4)*

Gravy for Foo Yung

1 tablespoon cornstarch	2 tablespoons soy sauce
2 tablespoons water	(or more to taste)
2 cups chicken stock	

Combine cornstarch and water to make a smooth paste; set aside. Combine stock and soy sauce in a small saucepan and heat. When stock begins to simmer, add a small amount of hot stock to the cornstarch mixture; stir and gradually add mixture to stock. Heat to boiling point, stirring constantly. When gravy has thickened, remove from heat and serve in gravy bowl to be poured over foo yung.

Pork Balls

This is a very delicately flavored dish that I like served over fine noodles.

2 pounds ground pork
4 teaspoons cornstarch
4 teaspoons soy sauce
4 teaspoons sherry
4 slices fresh ginger (each about
    1" across), minced, or ¼
    teaspoon powdered ginger

2 teaspoons honey
1 teaspoon vinegar
2 tablespoons sesame seeds

In a large bowl, combine all the ingredients listed above, and mix well. Form into balls about 1 inch in diameter. Steam the pork balls for 20 minutes, using as small an amount of water as possible so that the water from the steaming can be used as an accompanying sauce. Serve with soy sauce on the side. *(Serves 4)*

Simmered Pork

This is a full-flavored dish for which the meat is first marinated and then simmered in a sauce with sherry and ginger for almost two hours.

2 pounds lean pork	1 garlic clove
4 tablespoons soy sauce	1¼ cups water
1½ teaspoons sugar	1 cup sliced water chestnuts
1½ tablespoons dry sherry	4 scallions, cut in 1″ pieces
2 slices fresh ginger, minced, or	
⅛ teaspoon powdered	
ginger	

Cut the pork into bite-size pieces and set aside. Combine soy, sugar, sherry, ginger, and garlic, and pour over pork in a large bowl. Set aside to marinate for 20 minutes. Place pork and marinade in a large skillet. Cover meat with water, bring to a boil, and then reduce heat. Simmer covered for one hour, remove cover, and cook an additional 30 minutes. Add water chestnuts and scallion pieces, simmer an additional 3 minutes, and serve at once. *(Serves 4)*

Shredded Soy Chicken

If the chicken is just slightly frozen when you shred it, you'll find that it's much easier to cut. This dish cooks very quickly, but red pepper, scallions, and snow pea pods give it the appearance of a gourmet meal that takes hours to prepare.

2 cups shredded chicken, white
    meat
1 tablespoon cornstarch
1 lightly beaten egg white
6 tablespoons soy sauce
4 tablespoons dry sherry
1 tablespoon brown sugar
2 slices fresh ginger, minced, or
    ⅛ teaspoon powdered
    ginger

⅛ teaspoon black pepper
1 hot red fresh chili pepper or a
    pinch of flaked cayenne
    pepper
1 sweet red pepper
2 scallions
½ cup snow pea pods
4 tablespoons vegetable oil

Slice chicken as thin as possible, then cut into fine shreds no wider than ⅛". Sprinkle chicken pieces evenly with cornstarch and roll in beaten egg white to coat. Combine soy, sherry, sugar, ginger, black pepper, and red chili pepper to make a marinade. Pour marinade over chicken in a large bowl, and marinate for 20 minutes. While chicken marinates, remove seeds from sweet pepper; cut into thin slices. Cut scallions into 1" slices. Wash pea pods and set aside. When ready to cook, heat oil in a wok or large skillet. Drain marinade from chicken (save marinade) and stir-fry chicken for several minutes, until the meat is almost cooked through. Make a well in the center of the chicken pieces, add sweet pepper, scallions, and pea pods. Stir for one minute, then add marinade, and stir to coat meat and vegetables with sauce. Serve at once. *(Serves 4)*

Chicken with Walnuts and Peaches

Chicken together with fruit and nuts is a wonderful taste treat.

3 chicken breasts, skin and
  bones removed
2 tablespoons soy sauce
1 tablespoon dry sherry
1 teaspoon sugar

1 teaspoon cornstarch
½ cup chopped walnuts
3 tablespoons vegetable oil
⅛ teaspoon salt
1 cup sliced peaches

Dice chicken and set aside. Combine soy, sherry, sugar, and cornstarch, and pour over chicken in a large bowl. Set aside to marinate for 15 minutes. Meanwhile, heat oil in a wok or large skillet. Fry chopped walnuts in heated oil until they're golden brown. Remove nuts with slotted spoon, leaving oil in wok, and place on paper towels to drain. Sprinkle nuts with salt. Add chicken and marinade to the wok or skillet. Stir until chicken is cooked through, which should take less than 5 minutes. Add nuts and peaches, stirring just until the fruit is heated through. Serve at once. *(Serves 4)*

Chicken with Mixed Vegetables

2 cups diced white meat
   chicken
4 tablespoons soy sauce
2 tablespoons cornstarch
1 tablespoon vegetable oil
2 tablespoons sherry
1 teaspoon sugar
2 teaspoons hoisin sauce or
   smoke-flavored barbeque
   sauce

¼ cup chicken broth
2 slices fresh ginger, minced, or
   ⅛ teaspoon powdered
   ginger
¼ cup vegetable oil
6 scallions, in 1″ slices
2 cups pea sprouts
2 cups fresh mushrooms
½ cup cashews, chopped
   (optional)

Dice chicken and set aside. Combine soy, cornstarch, 1 tablespoon vegetable oil, sherry, sugar, hoisin sauce, chicken broth, and ginger to make marinade. Pour over chicken in large bowl, mix, and set aside for 20 minutes. To cook, heat ¼ cup oil in wok or large skillet. Drain chicken and reserve marinade. Add chicken to oil, and stir several minutes until chicken is almost cooked. Add scallions, sprouts, and mushrooms, stirring for one minute. Add marinade and stir to coat chicken and vegetables. If desired, add ½ cup chopped cashews, and serve. *(Serves 4–6)*

Special Roast Duck

The special secret for this duck, which is tender and juicy underneath a very crispy skin, is that the duck is filled with a hot broth
that has sherry and anise in it. The duck is roasted with the broth
inside its cavity, and afterward the broth is made into a rich sauce.

1 4–5 pound duck	⅛ teaspoon whole anise seed or
1 small onion	¼ teaspoon anise-flavored
1 tablespoon vegetable oil	extract
1 cup chicken broth	½ cup hot water
⅓ cup soy sauce	3 tablespoons honey
1 tablespoon sherry	2 tablespoons vinegar
1½ teaspoons sugar	4 teaspoons soy sauce
¼ teaspoon cinnamon	1 tablespoon cornstarch
	2 tablespoons water

Note: Most ducks have the skin from the neck folded quite
far underneath the body, which prevents liquids from escaping
through the neck cavity. For this dish, that's an absolute necessity.

Wash and dry the duck. Prick the skin all over with a sharp fork,
and set aside. Preheat oven to 425° F. Peel and chop the small onion
into small pieces. Heat 1 tablespoon oil in a medium-size skillet,

and sauté the onion in it until it's transparent. Add chicken broth, soy, sherry, sugar, cinnamon, and anise to the skillet. Cook until the liquid begins to simmer, and remove from heat. Pour the liquid into a large measuring cup or gravy boat, to make it easier to pour into the duck cavity. Hold the duck at an angle and pour the hot liquid into the cavity. With duck still held at an angle, close the opening and secure by sewing the edges of the cavity together. To prevent any liquid from escaping, bring one edge of skin over the opposite side to overlap; then bring up the tail and wrap thread over the tail to completely close the opening of the cavity. Put the duck onto a roasting rack inside a large roasting pan. Put ½ cup of hot water into the bottom of the roasting pan, reduce the oven heat to 325° F., and put the duck into the oven. Roast for ½ hour.

While the duck roasts, make a basting liquid of the honey, vinegar, and soy sauce. After ½ hour, baste the duck every 20 minutes until it's a dark, rich brown. (The duck should remain in the oven ½ hour for every pound. A four-pound duck takes 2 hours to roast, for example.) After one hour of roasting spoon the excess fat from the roasting pan, and either discard or save for frying other foods.

When the duck is finished, remove it from the roasting pan and cut open the strings securing the cavity. Carefully pour the liquid inside the duck into a small saucepan. Add remaining basting sauce to the pan, and bring liquid to a boil. While liquid heats, make a paste of 1 tablespoon cornstarch plus 2 tablespoons water. When the liquid begins to boil, gradually add the cornstarch paste, and stir constantly to make a sauce. Serve separately to pour over the carved duck pieces. *(Serves 2 if duck is served alone; serves 4 if another dish is also prepared)*

Steamed Sea Bass

1 2-pound sea bass, or 2 1-pound sea bass, depending on size of wok and availability of fish	2 tablespoons soy sauce
½ teaspoon salt	1 teaspoon cornstarch
¼ teaspoon black pepper	2 slices fresh ginger (about 1" across), in thin slivers, or
1 tablespoon vegetable oil	¼ teaspoon powdered ginger
½ cup water	1 tablespoon black beans
	2 scallions, cut into 1" slices

Wash and dry fish. Sprinkle both outside of fish and cavity with salt and pepper. Grease large wok or heavy skillet with vegetable oil. Place fish into wok. Combine water, soy, cornstarch, ginger, and black beans. Add sauce to wok, cover, and bring sauce to boil. Reduce heat and steam 15 minutes. Add scallion, steam additional 2 minutes, and serve. *(Serves 4, if served with another main dish; serves 2 if served alone)*

Sweet and Sour Sea Bass

Use fresh fish; leave the head and tail intact. This dish will be a masterpiece worthy of any special occasion.

1 2-pound sea bass	¼ cup sugar
2 tablespoons cornstarch	2 tablespoons vinegar
⅓ cup vegetable oil	3 tablespoons soy sauce
1 clove garlic	¼ cup water chestnuts, sliced
2 slices fresh ginger (about 1″	¼ cup sweet cucumber pickles
across), slivered, or ¼	½ cup snow pea pods
teaspoon powdered ginger	½ cup pineapple chunks
1 cup chicken stock	4 scallions, cut in 2″ pieces

Wash and dry fish; coat evenly with cornstarch. (It's all right to use two one-pound fish, if you prefer.) Score fish on both sides (make shallow incisions with a sharp knife every few inches), if you use one large fish. Heat oil in a large heavy skillet. When oil is hot, fry fish on both sides until it's crisp and brown and the flesh flakes when tested with chopsticks or a fork. Remove fish and set onto heated serving platter in very low oven. Sauté garlic and ginger in oil in skillet. Add stock, sugar, vinegar, and soy to pan, and stir over medium flame until hot. Add water chestnuts, pickles, pea pods, pineapple, scallion pieces; bring sauce to boil. Pour over fish and serve immediately. *(Serves 4 if served with another dish; serves 2 if served alone)*

Skewered Beef with Honey and Ginger

This dish becomes wonderfully full-flavored if you marinate the beef overnight. The sauce from the marinade is so good that you'll be tempted to eat it with a spoon.

2 pounds sirloin steak, 1" thick	2 slices fresh ginger, minced, or
½ cup vegetable oil	¼ teaspoon powdered
¼ cup soy sauce	ginger
3 tablespoons honey	2 garlic cloves
2 tablespoons vinegar	2 scallions, cut into 1" pieces
	skewers

Cut the steak into 1" cubes; remove excess fat. Combine the remaining ingredients to make a marinade. Pour over and mix with the beef in a large bowl. Marinate for several hours, or, if you can, overnight. When ready to cook, preheat the broiler. Skewer the steak pieces or simply place the meat directly under the broiler, basting often during the cooking process with the marinade. (Leave the scallions in the extra marinade; if you broil them, scallions will burn.) Broil the meat for several minutes on each side, and heat the extra marinade in a small saucepan. Serve with heated marinade as soon as the steak is cooked to your taste. *Serves 4)*

Szechuan Pepper Beef

This is fairly spicy. Even though the dried chili peppers used for Szechuan cooking are small, they're strong. For a milder dish, reduce the number of red chili peppers by half.

2 pounds lean beef	2 slices fresh ginger, minced,
4 tablespoons soy sauce	or ¼ teaspoon powdered
¼ teaspoon salt	ginger
4 tablespoons dry white wine	4 hot, dried, red chili peppers
¼ cup vegetable oil	2 scallions, cut into 1" slices
2 cloves garlic	

Cut beef into strips ¼" wide and several inches long. Combine soy, salt, and white wine to make a marinade. Pour marinade over beef in a large bowl, and set aside for 15 minutes. After meat has marinated, heat oil in a wok or large skillet. Sauté garlic, ginger, and red chili peppers for 2 minutes. Add beef (reserve marinade), and stir rapidly for several minutes until meat is cooked through. Add marinade and scallions, and heat for one minute. *(Serves 4)*

Almond Cookies

These are traditional cookies made with vegetable shortening, not butter. To be completely traditional, garnish the cookies by placing a drop of red food coloring in the center of each cookie. For an appealing variation, garnish each cookie with a whole unsalted almond.

1 cup vegetable shortening	2 drops yellow food coloring
1 cup sugar	½ teaspoon salt
2 eggs, beaten	3 cups sifted flour
1 teaspoon almond extract	2 egg whites
½ teaspoon vanilla extract	

Preheat oven to 350° F. Grease a large cookie sheet and set it aside. Cream together shortening and sugar; add beaten eggs and stir to combine. Add extracts, food coloring, and salt. Gradually add flour, stirring to form a stiff batter. You may use your hands to knead the dough. Shape dough into balls about 1″ in diameter. Dip balls into egg white, place 2″ apart on cookie sheet, and flatten with fingers. Garnish, if desired. Bake for 10 minutes, until cookies are light golden brown on top and browned on the bottom. *(Makes 48 cookies)*

French Cuisine

Introduction

I have worked and traveled all over the world. Of all the places I've been, the country that captured my heart more than any other was France. I love the combination of gracious cosmopolitan elegance and ageless charm of gentle rural beauty that I have found in Normandy, the province where I maintain my real home. When I'm on the road touring and performing on stage eight times a week, the thought of my home brings me comfort. And when I want to celebrate and have a night out on the town, wherever I am, I will seek out French cuisine.

There's no doubt about it: the French have a way with food. They treat everything that goes into a dish with genuine love and respect. Each ingredient is chosen with utmost care to ensure the best possible result. The French countryside is a greengrocer's dream, with fertile soil and moderate temperatures yielding nearly ideal crops season after season. Each French region or province has a specialty: chickens from Bresse, dairy products from Normandy, seafood from Brittany—fine wines from everywhere. And anyone

137

who can purchase only a few items sees the situation as a challenge, not a problem. Average French chefs don't merely cook, they invent incredible meals every time they set foot in the kitchen. Great French chefs create dishes that somehow coax food to new unparalleled heights. Their artistic genius is treated with tremendous respect. The famous chef Escoffier, for example, was given his own museum and was made an officer in the Legion of Honor after he invented peach Melba and tournedos Rossini. Of course, total obsession with perfection in any area can be a dangerous thing. There have been a few chefs who committed suicide when they felt they had failed in their culinary duties.

There are two distinct styles of French cooking. One is very basic and easy to master. Simple spicing, perhaps a little wine, nothing too complicated, and yet here before you is an incredible, mouthwatering dish. Coq au vin, for instance, is just chicken in wine sauce with mushrooms, onions, a hint of garlic, thyme, and bay leaf. One of the nicest shrimp dishes I've had is prepared by simply putting small shrimp, called grays, into cold water with salt and pepper to taste. The water is then brought to a boil and the shrimp are cooked for several minutes. If, by chance, a shrimp in the pot turns red, the dish is called a bouquet. The shrimp are eaten with a cider that is like a light white wine. In this culinary style a sort of magic really seems to be taking place in the cooking process.

Once you've learned how to prepare the basic French dishes, you'll be ready to try classic French foods. There are more rules to follow in classic cooking. The food has to be subtly seasoned, sauces must blend with the dish, not provide a contrasting flavor, and opposing tastes may never be mixed. You won't find, for example, a sweet and sour classic French dish. Certain ingredients immediately indicate that a recipe is in the classic tradition: natural juices, melted butter, heavy cream, wine, **foie gras**, and truffles. Foie gras is goose liver pâté, and truffles are wild fungi that grow in clusters on certain oak tree roots. The average truffle is the size of a walnut, and they're very, very expensive. François LaVarenne, a chef believed to have learned his craft in the Italian kitchens of the Medicis, is said to have introduced both truffles and mushrooms to the French cuisine. Mushrooms are widely considered elegant fare, and there are many kinds that can be quite delicious when properly prepared. In France, I've sampled fairy ring, ink, button, and yellow mushrooms.

It can take years to learn to make all of the sauces and stocks needed to cook classic French foods, and the easiest way to enjoy authentic haute cuisine, which requires hours of preparation for each meal, is simply to patronize a fine restaurant. The recipes I've chosen for this section, however, are easy to prepare at home without having to attend a cooking school. One of my favorite dishes, tournedos Rossini, is an example. It takes very little time and effort to prepare and it's the perfect dish to serve for any special occasion.

I've also selected many seafood dishes for this section. Normandy is a coastal province, and seafood practically swims from the ocean into waiting pots and pans. Mussels, clams, sole, turbot, brill, bluefish, snapper, scallops, shrimp—it's a fabulous place for fish fanciers. The beauty of the Normandy shore is complemented by a countryside covered with apple orchards and dairy farms. Local specialties are understandably often made with cream sauces that also contain either apple cider or apple brandy. Pork chops Normandes, for instance, combines heavy cream, fresh apple slices, and Calvados (apple brandy). Bluefish Normande is served with a sauce that contains cream, sweet butter, and hard apple cider. Calvados is also added to café au lait, and it's even sometimes brought to the table to be consumed straight, in a shot glass, at the middle of a meal. This is called "trou Normand," and it prepares your stomach for more food: it really does.

Trou Normand is a good cure to know about when you've finished your meal and want to have dessert. The only difficult thing about French sweets is choosing one over another. If you want to register a caloric complaint, you'll have to go back to Louis

XIV. He was the first monarch whose sweet tooth required daily feeding, and it was he who inspired the tradition of desserts as part of a meal. Our recipe selection ranges from coffee chocolate mousse to custard and fruit pies, from soufflé served with rum sauce to baked pears in wine, with other irresistibles, such as walnut pie and carrot cake, included for your final delight.

Include candlelight and a fine French wine with any of the following dishes, and you will be dining with me in my home.

Quiche

I love quiches because you can put practically anything into them and they'll come out of the oven looking like artwork. This recipe is for a fairly basic quiche, so that you can add your favorite vegetable or meat accordingly.

Pastry:

6 tablespoons butter	1 tablespoon vegetable oil
1½ cups flour	3–4 tablespoons milk

Melt the butter in a small saucepan. Combine flour, melted butter, and oil in a medium-size bowl. Gradually add milk until a moist dough is formed. (It's best to mix this dough with your hands.) Gather the dough into a ball. Roll the dough out on a floured board, and make a 10″ circle. Place circle into a 9″ pie pan, and prick the dough lightly with a fork. Set aside.

Filling:

6–8 bacon slices
 ¾ cup diced natural Swiss
   cheese
2 scallions
4 eggs

2 cups light cream
½ teaspoon salt
⅛ teaspoon white pepper
¼ cup minced black olives
¼ cup minced mushrooms

Preheat oven to 375° F. Cut bacon slices into 1" pieces, and fry in a small skillet until bacon is done but not overly crisp. Drain off fat and put bacon onto paper towel to drain completely; set aside. Dice cheese and mince the scallions. Sprinkle bacon, cheese, and scallion onto the bottom of the quiche crust. Beat the eggs lightly in a large bowl; add cream, salt, pepper, minced black olives, and minced mushrooms, and stir to combine ingredients. Pour the cream mixture into the pie plate, and bake at 375° F. for 40 minutes. Reduce oven temperature to 325° F. for an additional 20 minutes. To test for doneness, insert a toothpick into the center of the quiche. If the toothpick comes out clean, the quiche is ready. (*Serves 4 as a main dish, 6–8 as an appetizer*)

Caraway Cheese Soufflé

If you don't care for the flavor of caraway seeds, just eliminate them and you'll have a very simple and elegant cheese soufflé.

6 egg whites	Dash nutmeg
3 egg yolks°	1 small bay leaf
3 tablespoons butter	½ cup grated natural Swiss
3 tablespoons flour	cheese
1 cup milk	¼ cup grated Parmesan cheese
Dash of cayenne pepper	½ teaspoon caraway seeds

Butter a 7″ soufflé dish and dust the buttered dish with flour. Preheat the oven to 375° F. Beat the egg whites to stiff peaks and set aside. Beat the egg yolks in a separate bowl and set aside. Melt the butter in a medium-size saucepan. Remove the pan from the heat after the butter has melted, and gradually whisk in the flour so that no lumps form. Next slowly add the milk to the pan, whisking the mixture constantly. When the milk is thoroughly blended with the butter and flour, add the cayenne, nutmeg, and bay leaf. Return the pan to a moderate heat, and continue whisking while the liquid comes to a boil. As soon as the boiling point is reached, remove the pan from the heat. Remove the bay leaf, and gradually add, first, the two cheeses and then the beaten egg yolk to the pan, using a whisk to combine the ingredients. Next whisk ⅓ of the stiff egg whites into the soufflé mixture. Add the caraway seeds, and fold in the remaining egg whites, using as few strokes as possible so that the egg whites are mixed into the soufflé but not completely deflated. Gently pour the mixture into the soufflé dish and bake for 20 to 25 minutes. The soufflé will appear golden on top when it's done, and the flour and butter from the soufflé dish will form a coating around the sides of the soufflé. Serve as soon as the dish is cooked. *(Serves 4)*

°Extra egg yolks may be reserved for next day's breakfast.

Creamy Liver Pâté

You may want to try a young beaujolais, called beaujolais nouveau, with your pâté. In France, if the new beaujolais has an exceptionally good flavor when it's tasted for the first time, that is taken as a sign that the coming year will also be exceptional in many ways.

This particular pâté combines liver with heavy cream, butter, cognac, spices, and apple for a very rich yet surprisingly light flavor. I like to serve fresh thin apple slices, creamy muenster cheese, and French bread along with the pâté.

1 pound calves liver	¾ teaspoon salt
4 tablespoons vegetable oil	⅛ teaspoon black pepper
2 tablespoons butter	½ teaspoon nutmeg
1 carrot, finely minced	¼ cup heavy cream
1 small onion, finely minced	¼ pound butter
1 small apple, peeled, cored and sliced	3–4 tablespoons cognac
	4 tablespoons melted butter
1 tablespoon fresh parsley or ½ teaspoon dried parsley	

Butter a 1–1½ quart pâté mold or oblong casserole dish and set aside. Wash liver and cut into small pieces, removing any membranes. Heat oil in a large, heavy skillet. Sauté liver for several minutes until it's dark on the outside but still slightly pink on the inside. Remove from the oil and set aside. Melt 2 tablespoons of butter in the same skillet. Sauté the carrot and onion until the onion is transparent. (A food processor is ideal for mincing the vegetables.) Combine the sautéed vegetables, butter, and pan drippings with the liver. Gradually purée this mixture a bit at a time in a food processor. Add the apple slices and seasonings. Gradually add the heavy cream and butter. Whip the pâté until it's quite fluffy. Add the cognac and pour pâté into the mold. Melt 4 tablespoons of butter and pour over the top of the pâté. Cover and refrigerate overnight before serving. *(Serves 8 as appetizer)*

Coquilles St. Jacques

What could be better than fresh scallops in a white wine and cream sauce? This dish is wonderful served with a crisp green salad for a main dish or as an appetizer all by itself. This is also excellent with shrimp instead of scallops.

1½ pounds fresh scallops	1 cup heavy cream
4 tablespoons butter	3 tablespoons flour
¼ cup minced onion	6 tablespoons water
1 cup chopped mushrooms	Dash cayenne pepper
1 cup dry white wine	½ cup grated Parmesan cheese

Butter a large, shallow baking dish; set aside. Wash scallops, and cut any large scallops in half. Melt butter in a large skillet. Sauté scallops lightly on all sides for a few minutes—they don't take very long to cook. Remove and set aside. Sauté minced onion and chopped mushrooms in the same skillet until onions are transparent. Add the wine and simmer for 3 minutes. Add the heavy cream and simmer gently. Combine the flour and water to make a smooth paste. Add some of the hot cream-wine mixture to the paste. Bring the liquid in the pan to the boiling point. Add the paste to the boiling liquid gradually, while stirring rapidly, so that the liquid thickens into a sauce. As soon as the sauce thickens, reduce heat and simmer gently. Add the scallops to the pan after the sauce has reduced slightly in quantity. Simmer to heat scallops through, then pour mixture into the baking dish. Preheat the broiler. Add a dash of cayenne pepper to the grated Parmesan cheese. Sprinkle the top of the scallops with the cheese, and place under the broiler for a few minutes until the cheese melts and is a light golden brown. Serve at once. *(Serves 8 as appetizer or 4 as main dish)*

Vichyssoise

Vichyssoise is made with a very rich chicken stock. You may prepare your own from the following recipe or use commercially prepared stock.

Chicken Stock:

1 small chicken, cut into pieces	2 celery stalks, tops included
Giblets from chicken	1 large bay leaf
2 small onions	6 cups water
2 carrots	

Wash chicken and giblets; place into large soup kettle. Peel onions, slice carrots and celery, and add to pot. Add bay leaf and cover with 6 cups water. Simmer for several hours, skimming residue that rises to the surface. After the stock is reduced to about 4 cups, strain and use for vichyssoise. Cooked chicken may be used for salad, sandwiches, or in casseroles.

Soup:

4 tablespoons sweet butter	4 cups chicken stock
1 medium onion, chopped	1 cup heavy cream
2 celery stalks, chopped	½ teaspoon salt
2 medium white potatoes,	Fresh black pepper
peeled, sliced thinly	Fresh parsley

Melt butter in a soup kettle. Add chopped onion and celery, and sauté until the vegetables are soft. Add the peeled, sliced white potatoes and chicken stock. Simmer until the potatoes are cooked through. Remove from heat and cool. Purée mixture in blender or food processor. Add cream and salt. Chill and serve garnished with a sprinkling of freshly ground black pepper and fresh parsley. *(Serves 4)*

Onion Soup

If you wish, you may use a commercially prepared stock for this soup, or use the recipe given above for chicken stock to make the stock for onion soup, adding an additional cup of water during the cooking process. If you find that there is a great quantity of chicken fat on the top of the stock, you may remove some of it very easily by waiting until the stock has cooled some but is still quite warm. Then add a cup of crushed ice all at once to the stock. The fat will harden and you can simply lift it from the surface of the stock. If stock was prepared a day or so in advance and chilled, the congealed fat may be lifted off easily.

6 tablespoons sweet butter	4 tablespoons Parmesan cheese
3 cups thinly sliced sweet onions	¼ pound muenster or Jarlsberg Swiss cheese
5 cups chicken stock	Salt and pepper
4 slices French bread	

Melt 4 tablespoons of the butter in a large, heavy skillet. Sauté sliced onions until transparent, and then remove from heat. Put stock into a soup kettle. Add onions and the butter in which the onions were cooked. Simmer, to combine flavors, for 30 minutes. While soup simmers, spread French bread slices with remaining 2 tablespoons butter, and sprinkle evenly with Parmesan cheese— 1 tablespoon cheese to each bread slice. Place under broiler until cheese is golden brown. Set bread aside. Adjust oven temperature to 375° F. Divide the soup into 4 heavy small onion soup crocks. Place a bread slice on top of each crock. Divide the muenster or Swiss cheese into 4 equal parts; place over bread, and bake in the oven until the cheese has melted and is light golden brown. *(Serves 4)*

Cream of Carrot Soup

This wonderful soup is perfect for special occasions; it contains heavy cream and sherry and is very rich.

2 tablespoons butter	½ cup sherry
1 cup chopped celery	¾ cup cooked rice
½ cup chopped onion	1 cup heavy cream
4 cups chicken stock	Salt and pepper
2 cups thinly sliced carrots	

Melt butter in a small skillet. Add chopped celery and onion, and sauté until the vegetables are soft. Put stock into a soup kettle. Add sautéed celery and onion, sliced carrots, and simmer until carrots are soft. Add sherry, and simmer an additional 15 minutes. Remove soup from heat, cool it, and purée in blender or food processor. Reheat soup slowly, and, when soup begins to simmer, add cooked rice and heavy cream. When rice is heated through, season to taste with salt and pepper, and serve. *(Serves 6)*

Light Salad Dressing

I like this dressing very much because it allows the flavor of the salad greens to come through. If you use a soft lettuce, such as Bibb or Boston, use slightly less vinegar.

5 tablespoons vegetable oil	2 fresh shallots
1 tablespoon red wine vinegar	Celery salt

Combine oil and vinegar in a small jar with a tight-fitting lid. Put the bulbs of the shallots into a garlic press; squeeze the shallots so that the juice runs into the jar with the oil and vinegar. Close the jar and shake well. Season to taste with celery salt, mix again, and toss with one small head of your favorite lettuce. *(Serves 4)*

Vinaigrette Salad Dressing

This version of oil and vinegar dressing is brightened by a touch of lemon juice. I think it's best when made just before you mix the salad.

5 tablespoons olive or vegetable oil
2 tablespoons red wine vinegar
¼ teaspoon Dijon mustard
½ teaspoon lemon juice
¼ teaspoon salt

Dash of freshly ground black pepper
1 tablespoon minced fresh parsley or ¼ teaspoon dried parsley

Combine all of the above in a container with a tightly fitting lid. Shake vigorously to combine, and toss with choice of salad greens. *(Serves 4)*

Roquefort Salad Dressing

This rich and flavorful dressing is perfect when served with the following watercress and endive salad.

½ cup olive oil
⅛ cup red wine vinegar
½ teaspoon tarragon
⅛ teaspoon freshly ground black pepper
Dash salt

2 tablespoons minced fresh parsley
¼ cup crumbled Roquefort cheese
2 tablespoons heavy cream

Combine oil, vinegar, tarragon, pepper, salt, and parsley in a container with a tightly fitting lid. Shake well, and then add crumbled cheese. Stir in cream, and serve with watercress and endive salad, below. *(Serves 8)*

Watercress and Endive Salad

This salad is good with Roquefort Salad Dressing (page 149) or with Light Salad Dressing (page 148). Either toss salad ingredients together with the dressing, or, for each serving, arrange the following on a small salad plate, then pour a little dressing over each salad.

4 endive leaves
2 slices of sweet apple, cored
    but not peeled

1 small bunch of watercress

Mushrooms with Cream

This is a tasty appetizer if served on toast. It is also a marvelous side dish.

4 tablespoons sweet butter
4–5 cups fresh mushrooms
½ cup dry white wine
½ cup heavy cream
¼ teaspoon salt

⅛ teaspoon white pepper
1 tablespoon fresh parsley or
    ¼ teaspoon dried parsley
8 slices French bread, toasted
    and buttered

Melt butter in a heavy skillet. Slice mushrooms and sauté in melted butter over low heat for several minutes. Add wine and simmer for 5 minutes. Stir in cream and seasonings. Heat through and simmer. When sauce has reduced slightly, serve on hot, toasted, buttered French bread if serving as appetizer. If serving as a side dish, simply put cooked mushrooms into a heated serving bowl and bring directly to the table. *(Serves 6 as appetizer, 4 as side dish)*

Ratatouille

Ratatouille is excellent served as a side dish, inside an omelette, or as a meatless main dish.

1 green pepper	1 garlic clove
1 medium onion	½ cup water
1 medium eggplant	½ teaspoon basil
1 small zucchini squash	½ teaspoon salt
3 medium tomatoes	¼ teaspoon black pepper
½ cup fresh mushrooms	12 green olives, pimento stuffed
¼ cup vegetable oil	(optional)

Remove seeds and veins from green pepper, and cut pepper into thin strips. Peel and slice the onion into thin slices. Peel and slice the eggplant into ¼" slices. Slice the zucchini into ¼" slices. Quarter the tomatoes and slice the mushrooms. Heat vegetable oil in a heavy saucepan. Sauté the garlic clove in the oil, then add the pepper and onion and sauté several minutes. Add sliced eggplant, zucchini, and tomatoes. Add water and seasonings, cover, and simmer over low heat for 40 minutes. Add mushrooms and simmer an additional 15 minutes. Add olives, if desired, and simmer until olives are heated through. *(Serves 6)*

Braised Endive

The full flavor of endive is softened by a sauce made of butter, lemon, sugar, and chicken stock.

6 bunches of endive	1 tablespoon lemon juice
4 tablespoons butter	1 teaspoon sugar
¼ cup chicken stock	Salt

Wash bunches of endive and remove and discard outer leaves. Set remaining endive aside to dry. Melt butter in a large skillet, and brown endive lightly on all sides. Combine stock, lemon juice, and sugar; pour liquid over endive. Reduce heat, cover skillet, and simmer about 20 minutes or until endive is tender. Season to taste with salt. *(Serves 4)*

Crisp-Fried Eggplant

You can substitute zucchini squash or asparagus that has been partially steamed for eggplant in this recipe. (Also try frying sweet potatoes in oil; they're a different accompaniment to a meal and a nice surprise when you're used to french fried white potatoes.)

1 large eggplant	Pepper
½ cup unseasoned bread crumbs	2 eggs
	Vegetable oil in a deep-fat
½ cup grated Parmesan cheese	fryer
¼ teaspoon salt	1 fresh lemon

Peel the eggplant and cut it into slices no thicker than ⅓". Cut each slice into strips no thicker than ⅓", so that you have slices of vegetable resembling french fries. Combine bread crumbs, Parmesan cheese, and salt and pepper to taste in a large shallow bowl. Place the vegetable pieces in another large shallow bowl. Beat the eggs and pour them over the eggplant slices, gently turning the eggplant so that the egg is evenly distributed. Sprinkle the bread crumb mixture over the egg-covered eggplant and roll the pieces of eggplant to be sure each slice is coated well. Place breaded eggplant in the refrigerator to chill while you heat vegetable oil in a deep-fat fryer. When oil is hot, fry eggplant in several batches. Drain on paper towels. Serve with slices of fresh lemon. *(Serves 4)*

Fluffy Baked Omelette

Beaten egg whites are folded into egg yolks to create a light, airy omelette that is first cooked in a pan on top of the stove and then placed into the oven to rise.

4 large eggs	Pepper
2 tablespoons water	½ tablespoon butter
Salt	

Preheat oven to 350° F. Separate yolks and whites of eggs, placing each into two separate bowls. Beat egg whites until stiff; set aside. Beat yolks with water, add a dash of salt and pepper, then fold egg whites into yolks. Melt butter in an omelette pan. Gently pour egg mixture into pan, and cook over a low heat for about 1 minute. Place pan into preheated oven, and cook for 5–6 minutes until eggs are set and omelette has risen. Remove pan from oven, fold omelette in half, and serve. *(Serves 2)*

Omelette Fillings

Place the cooked, heated filling of your choice on one half of the omelette during the last several minutes of baking. I like the ratatouille mentioned in this section inside an omelette. Try any combination that you like: ham, bacon, cheese, vegetables or sweet dessert fillings such as whipped cream or cream cheese with jams or fresh fruit. (Whipped cream goes into the omelette just before serving.)

Coq Au Vin

This is one of the oldest, most traditional of French meals—a simple dish of chicken cooked in red wine.

6 tablespoons butter	3 small bay leaves
4 pounds of chicken breasts and legs	1½ cups dry red wine
	½ cup chicken stock
12 small onions, peeled	1 cup sliced mushrooms
2 garlic cloves	½ teaspoon salt
½ teaspoon thyme	¼ teaspoon black pepper
½ teaspoon sweet basil	¼ teaspoon nutmeg

Preheat oven to 325° F. In a Dutch oven on top of the stove, melt 6 tablespoons butter. Add chicken pieces, browning each piece on both sides. Add onions, garlic, thyme, basil, bay leaves, wine, and chicken stock. Bring slowly to a boil, cover, and place in oven for one hour. Then add mushrooms, salt, pepper, and nutmeg. Return to oven for an additional 15 minutes. Serve with small boiled white potatoes, and crisp French bread to dip into the sauce. *(Serves 4)*

Stuffed Rock Cornish Game Hen

The dressing for this dish is made with rice. You only need to add a vegetable and salad to have a complete delicious meal.

4 hens, about 1½ pounds each	4 slices bacon

Wash and dry hens. Set aside and preheat oven to 350° F.

Dressing:

4 tablespoons sweet butter	⅛ teaspoon black pepper
½ cup chopped celery	2 cups cooked rice
½ cup chopped mushrooms	½ cup bread crumbs
1 medium onion, minced	1 tablespoon milk
½ cup raisins	¼ teaspoon nutmeg
¼ teaspoon salt	

Melt butter in a large skillet. Sauté celery, mushrooms, and onion in butter until onion is transparent. Add raisins, salt, and pepper. Transfer mixture to a large bowl, and combine with rice and bread crumbs. Moisten with milk and add nutmeg. Stir well and stuff hens with dressing. *(Makes enough dressing for 4 Cornish hens)*

After hens are stuffed, place then on a baking rack set inside a large roasting pan. Cut the bacon slices in half, and place two halves of bacon on top of each hen. Roast uncovered for about 50 minutes. Then remove bacon and baste frequently with honey glaze (recipe follows); roast an additional 15–20 minutes, until well browned. *(Serves 4)*

Honey Glaze

This glaze is excellent on any game bird; try it on roast duckling as well as on the game hens.

½ cup honey   Dash of powdered cloves
6 tablespoons dry red wine

Stir the honey and wine together in a small bowl until they are well mixed. Add a dash of powdered cloves, and brush over the surface of game hens or duck as directed. *(Makes enough glaze for 1 large bird or 2 small birds)*

Roast Duckling

Allow one 5-pound duck for every 2 people served. Wash and dry the ducks. Place inside each duck cavity:

1 cored apple, cut into quarters   1 celery stalk, cut in half
2 small onions, peeled

(The apple and vegetables are discarded after roasting; they are used to reduce the "gamey" flavor sometimes associated with duckling.)

Preheat the oven to 400° F. Prick the skin of the duck lightly all over with a sharp fork to release the duck fat as it melts during roasting. Put the duckling on a roasting rack inside a roasting pan, and place in preheated oven. Reduce heat to 350° F. After one hour, pour off accumulated duck fat. Continue roasting another hour. Remove duck from oven, and let stand 5 minutes before carving. Serve with wild rice, any of the following sauces, or with glazed apple slices. *(Serves 2 for each 5-pound duck)*

Sauces

Either make a duck stock for the sauce recipes or substitute commercially prepared chicken stock for duck stock.

Duck Stock (made from one duck; if using two, double ingredients):

Giblets and neck from duck, small amount of fat from inside cavity
1 carrot, thinly sliced
1 celery stalk, sliced in thin pieces

1 onion, peeled and cut in half
1 clove garlic
1 large bay leaf
2 cups water

Wash giblets and neck and put with fat into a small saucepan. Add sliced carrot and celery, onion, garlic, and bay leaf. Cover with 2 cups of water, and simmer gently until stock is reduced to about one cup. Remove any residue which rises to the top, strain stock, and set aside.

Orange Sauce:

1 cup duck stock
Juice from 1 navel orange
1 tablespoon vinegar
1 tablespoon sugar
2 tablespoons orange marmalade

Dash powdered cloves
Dash salt
1 tablespoon flour
2 tablespoons water
1 tablespoon Grand Marnier

Combine stock, orange juice, vinegar, sugar, marmalade, cloves, and salt in a small saucepan. Bring to a boil, then reduce heat and simmer 15 minutes so that liquid is reduced. While sauce simmers, combine flour and water to make a smooth paste (roux). Add a bit of the hot sauce to the roux, stir, and add the mixture to the sauce in the pan. Stir constantly, and, when sauce has reached desired thickness, add Grand Marnier. Simmer another few minutes, and then remove from heat. (For a thinner sauce, simply add less roux.) If you wish, you may add pan drippings to the sauce. *(Makes enough sauce for 1 five-pound duck)*

Cherry Sauce:

If you prefer peaches, apricots, or plums to cherries, by all means substitute them in the following recipe.

1 cup pitted Bing cherries	Dash of salt
¼ cup brandy	1 tablespoon flour
1 teaspoon sugar	2 tablespoons water
1 cup duck stock (see page 158)	1 tablespoon kirsch

Marinate cherries in brandy and sugar for one hour. Place duck stock and salt into a small saucepan. Bring to boil, reduce heat, and simmer about 20 minutes to slightly reduce amount of stock. Add the cherries and brandy to the saucepan, and simmer for 5 minutes. While stock simmers, prepare a roux with the flour and water as directed in the preceding orange sauce recipe. Thicken the sauce by adding a bit of the hot sauce to the paste, and then adding the mixture back into the sauce until sauce is as thick as you prefer. Bring sauce to a boil, add kirsch, reduce heat, simmer for several minutes, and serve. *(Makes enough sauce for 1 five-pound duck)*

Glazed Apple Slices

These are the perfect accompaniment to roast duckling, whether you choose to also make a sauce or serve the duck plain. (They're also good with vanilla ice cream for dessert.)

6 small cooking apples	Dash of powdered cloves
(MacIntosh are nice)	¼ cup raisins
¾ cup maple syrup	Pinch of salt
¼ cup orange juice	2 tablespoons butter
¼ teaspoon cinnamon	

If cooking separately, preheat oven to 350° F. If cooking with roast duckling, place into oven with duck for 25–30 minutes. Peel, core, and slice apples. Butter a shallow baking dish, and place apples into the dish. Combine syrup, honey, orange juice, cinnamon, cloves, raisins, and salt; pour over apples. Dot with 2 tablespoons butter, and bake as directed above, turning apples after 15 minutes so they cook evenly. *(Serves 4)*

Pot Roast Provençale

This is a rich, hearty dish that's very good with a full-bodied red wine. It also produces a generous amount of savory sauce that you can spoon over the meat after you thicken it into gravy.

1 3-pound chuck, rump, or bottom round of beef	2 medium onions, peeled and cut in half
1 garlic clove	1 large bay leaf
4 tablespoons bacon fat or vegetable oil	¾ cup beef stock
	¾ cup dry red wine
2 carrots, cut into 1" slices	2 tablespoons flour
1 celery stalk, cut in 2" slices	4 tablespoons water
	Salt and pepper

Rub the meat with garlic, then discard garlic. In a large Dutch oven, melt the bacon fat, add meat, and brown on all sides. Finish with meat turned so that the side with the most fat is on the top. Add carrot slices, celery slices, onions, bay leaf, stock, and red wine. Bring to boil, reduce heat, and simmer covered for 3–3½ hours. After 1½ hours, check amount of liquid. If desired, add more stock or wine. When meat is cooked, lift it out and set aside. Make a roux (paste of flour and water). Bring the broth in the Dutch oven to a boil, and slowly add the roux, stirring rapidly so that a gravy is formed. Simmer gently for a few minutes, and then remove from heat. Season to taste with salt and pepper. Slice meat and serve with the gravy. *(Serves 4)*

Roulades de Boeuf

These stuffed rolls of beef are very tender. They're simmered in a red wine sauce and filled with a veal dressing.

1 2-pound flank steak	⅛ teaspoon salt
2 tablespoons vegetable oil	Dash of black pepper
1 garlic clove	8 cornichon (optional)
1 medium onion, chopped	1 cup hot beef stock
½ pound ground veal	1 cup dry red wine
½ cup bread crumbs	2 tablespoons tomato paste
½ carrot, shredded	4 tablespoons butter
1 egg	

Pound flank steak into a very large, thin rectangle, large enough to cut 8 rectangles about 3″ x 4″ and about ⅛″ thick. Heat oil in a large skillet. Sauté garlic and onion until the onion is transparent; set aside. In a large bowl, mix together ground veal, bread crumbs, carrot, egg, salt, and pepper. Divide the resulting dressing into 8 equal parts, and make finger-shaped cylinders. If you wish, place a cornichon into the center of each cylinder of dressing. Put the dressing into the middle of the beef rectangles, fold over the edges, and fold in the sides to make a sealed meat envelope. Set stuffed beef aside. Combine stock, wine, and tomato paste. Melt the butter in the large skillet with the onion and garlic. Add the beef roulades and sauté briefly on each side. Cover with the stock mixture, put a lid on the skillet, and cook covered for 1¼ hours, turning roulades once during the middle of the cooking time. *(Serves 4)*

Steak au Poivre

The sauce that goes with this steak is so very delicious that your guests will think you spent all day in the kitchen preparing it; you don't have to tell them it takes only minutes.

2 tablespoons crushed black peppercorns (more or less to taste)	5 tablespoons sweet butter
	2 tablespoons minced scallion
	¾ cup beef stock
4 shell steaks, ¾" thick (sirloin may be used, too)	¼ cup dry red wine
	3 tablespoons cognac
1 tablespoon vegetable oil	

Press crushed peppercorns into both sides of the meat, using the palm of your hand, and set aside for 15–20 minutes. Then heat oil and 3 tablespoons of the butter in a large skillet. Sauté the meat to individual taste, place on warm platter, and put in a warm oven while you quickly make the sauce. First add another tablespoon of butter to the skillet, and sauté the scallion. Combine stock and wine, add to skillet, and bring liquid to boil. Boil for one minute, add cognac, and boil one more minute. Add last tablespoon of the sweet butter, stir until butter melts and then pour sauce over the steaks, and serve at once. *(Serves 4)*

Tournedos Rossini

Truffles are the traditional garnish for tournedos Rossini. Since they're so expensive, however, I've found that you may substitute a single large black olive, cut in half, for each truffle. The olive gives the dish the color of the truffle and tastes fine in combination with the beef. You may also use foie gras that has been made with truffles if you wish, and then you will have all the proper ingredients for an authentic tournedo Rossini.

4 slices firm round white bread	4 slices black truffle or 4 black
8 tablespoons butter	olives (see note above)
4 center cut filets mignons	1 cup beef stock or gravy
1½"–2" thick	½ cup port wine
Salt and pepper	
4 slices foie gras or the pâté of	
your choice	

Toast bread slices and then cool. Generously butter cooled toast, and place under broiler until butter melts into the toast. (I like bread cut from a fresh loaf so that the slices are about ½" thick and as large around as the meat.) Set toast slices aside. In a large skillet, melt most of the remaining butter, reserving 2 tablespoons. Sprinkle filets with salt and pepper; sauté about 5–6 minutes on each side, turning several times. (Ideally, the meat should be rare to medium-rare for this dish.) While meat cooks, place toast slices on serving platter. When meat is done, place each filet on a toast slice. Put a slice of foie gras on each filet, and then a slice of truffle, or black olive sliced in half. Add the stock and wine to the skillet that you used to cook the beef. Heat to boiling point while stirring, then reduce heat, and add reserved 2 tablespoons of butter. When butter has melted, stir, and pour sauce over filets, and serve at once. *(Serves 4)*

Blanquette de Veau l'Ancienne

In this recipe, you may substitute chicken for the high-priced veal. Whether you choose chicken or veal, the result is an elegant dish suitable for any very special event.

24 small white onions
4 large carrots
6 pounds veal stew meat (or cubes of chicken)
4 cups beef broth (or chicken broth, if using chicken)
1 teaspoon thyme
1 teaspoon parsley or 1 tablespoon fresh parsley
1 teaspoon rosemary
5" square of cheesecloth
3 tablespoons flour
3 tablespoons milk

3 tablespoons sauce from pan
¼ pound sweet butter, melted
1 teaspoon nutmeg
3 egg yolks, slightly beaten
1 pound fresh mushrooms, large white, gently washed and dried
1 cup light cream
1 bay leaf
Salt and pepper to taste
2 fresh lemons, cut in wedges
2 tablespoons fresh parsley

Peel onions; set aside. Julienne carrots; set aside. Wash veal and put into a large Dutch oven. Add broth, bring to boil, reduce heat, and simmer for 5 minutes. While veal simmers, combine thyme, parsley, and rosemary in the cheesecloth. Gather the edges of the cloth together, and tie securely so the herbs can't escape. Add the resulting bouquet garni to the Dutch oven, and put the prepared vegetables on top of the meat. Cover and cook slowly for one hour and 45 minutes. At the end of the cooking time, make a roux by blending together in a small bowl the flour, milk, and pan sauce. In a separate bowl, combine melted butter, which has been allowed to cool, with nutmeg and three slightly beaten egg yolks. Next, place mushrooms into a saucepan with the light cream and bay leaf. Put over low heat, and let the mushrooms cook gently while you thicken the sauce from the meat, as follows.

Place the meat on a serving platter. Arrange the carrots and onions over the meat or next to the meat, as you wish. Place platter in a warm oven. Bring the sauce in the Dutch oven to a boil. Add roux to the sauce, constantly stirring so lumps don't form. When gravy is thickened to your preference, lower heat and add butter, nutmeg, and egg yolk mixture. Stir and heat through, but do not boil. Drain the cream from the mushrooms, and put the mushrooms around the edge of the meat. Pour some of the gravy over the meat and vegetables on the serving platter, and serve the remaining gravy separately. Serve with salt and pepper to taste and with fresh lemon wedges. Garnish with fresh parsley. *(Serves 6)*

Roast Leg of Lamb

Serve this marinated roast when its internal temperature is 155–160° F., so that the meat is slightly pink.

1 3-pound leg of lamb	1 bay leaf
½ cup olive oil	½ teaspoon basil
⅓ cup lemon juice	½ teaspoon thyme
1 large garlic clove, minced	

Remove outer skin and excess fat from leg of lamb. Combine remaining ingredients and marinate lamb overnight. When ready to roast, preheat oven to 350° F. Roast lamb 30 minutes for each pound. During roasting, baste with marinade. *(Serves 4)*

Mint Sauce

If you're in an adventurous frame of mind, try this sauce with the roast lamb instead of the usual mint jelly.

¼ cup minced mint leaves (fresh, if possible)	2 tablespoons sugar
¼ cup vinegar	2 tablespoons fresh lemon juice
3 tablespoons water	1 teaspoon mustard (Pommery is particularly good)

Just before the lamb is ready to serve, mix together all of the above, and serve in a separate container so that your guests may help themselves.

Pork Chops Normandes

Pork and apples, cooked together with cream and calvados, combine to make an easy but mouth-watering Dutch oven dinner.

2 tablespoons sweet butter	2 tablespoons cornstarch
2 shallots, minced or two	4 tablespoons water
onions, minced	¼ cup Calvados
4 loin pork chops	1 cup heavy cream
1 cup chicken stock	Salt and pepper
1 large sweet apple, peeled,	Fresh parsley
cored and sliced	

Melt butter in a Dutch oven. Saucé shallots. Add pork chops and brown lightly on both sides. Add chicken stock; cover and simmer for 1 hour. Add apple slices and simmer an additional 30 minutes. While dish simmers, mix cornstarch with water to make a paste (roux). Remove pork and apple slices from sauce and place onto serving platter. Place in warm oven. Add calvados to liquid in Dutch oven, and bring to a boil. Gradually add roux, stirring constantly, until sauce thickens. Reduce heat and add cream, and gradually bring to the boiling point once more. Remove from heat immediately, and pour some of the sauce over pork and apples on serving platter. Serve extra sauce separately. Season to individual taste with salt and pepper, garnish with fresh parsley, and serve at once. *(Serves 4)*

Fillet of Sole

Use fresh fish, if at all possible. Fillets of sole are small; serve 2 for each person, and season after cooking with salt and pepper. See following recipe for garnish.

12 fillets of sole
6 tablespoons sweet butter

Remove the broiler tray from your oven. Preheat the broiler for five minutes. Cover the broiler tray with aluminum foil. Place the sole on the foil, leaving a bit of space between each fillet. Broil for 3 minutes with the tray about 4" from the source of heat. Pull the tray out and dot each fillet with sweet butter. Cook for another 30 seconds only, just to melt the butter. Carefully remove fillets with spatula, place on a serving platter, and sprinkle with the juice of the lemons. Garnish with parsley tops sautéed in sweet butter, using the following recipe. (Prepare while broiling the fillets.) *(Serves 6)*

Parsley Tops in Sweet Butter

This must be made with fresh parsley.

4–6 tablespoons sweet butter   **¾–1 cup fresh parsley (tops only)**

Melt the butter slowly in a small skillet. Cut fresh parsley tops from their stalks; sauté in melted butter until parsley has lightly browned. Pour over fillets of sole or serve with the following recipe for dover sole.

Dover Sole

For this simple recipe, the trick is in cooking with an unskinned, cleaned, whole fish, head and tail intact. If you like, season to taste after cooking with salt and pepper.

4 1-pound whole Dover soles	1–2 fresh lemons
Clarified butter	

Wash and dry fish. Brush each side of each fish with clarified butter. Cook the fish on top of the stove in a nonstick surface frying pan for about 4 minutes on each side, using a moderate heat. (Fish is done when flesh flakes easily when tested with a fork.) Sprinkle cooked fish with fresh lemon juice, and serve with sautéed parsley tops. *(Serves 4)*

Sole Veronique

Sole with a sauce of heavy cream and white grapes; simply perfect.

3 tablespoons flour
¼ teaspoon salt
⅛ teaspoon ground black
    pepper
½ teaspoon tarragon
2 tablespoons fresh minced
    parsley
2 pounds fresh sole fillets
1 tablespoon butter

½ cup dry white wine
2 tablespoons flour
4 tablespoons water
1 cup heavy cream
1 egg yolk
  Salt to taste
1 cup fresh seedless white
    grapes
  Fresh parsley sprigs

Preheat oven to 400° F. Combine 3 tablespoons flour with salt, pepper, tarragon, and minced parsley. Coat fish with flour mixture. Butter a large, shallow baking dish, and place fish in a single layer into the dish. Add the wine and place the dish into the oven. Bake about 10–12 minutes, or until the fish flakes when tested with a fork. While the fish bakes, combine 2 tablespoons of flour with 4 tablespoons water to make a roux (paste). Heat the cream over a very low flame. Beat the egg yolk and add a small amount of heated cream to the egg; then slowly add the egg mixture to the hot cream. Next gradually add the roux, stirring constantly until the sauce thickens to your taste. Add salt to taste and the grapes to the sauce and heat through. Arrange cooked fish on a serving platter and pour the sauce over the fish. Garnish with fresh parsley sprigs, and serve. *(Serves 4)*

Broiled Salmon

I enjoy broiled salmon with a sour cream sauce (below), which can be served hot or cold, according to individual taste.

4 tablespoons butter   **4 salmon steaks**

Preheat broiler. Dot one side of each salmon steak with half of the butter. Broil for several minutes; turn and cover with remaining butter. While salmon broils on the second side, make the sauce. *(Serves 4)*

Sour Cream Lemon Sauce

This sauce is good with any rich tasting fish.

1 cup sour cream	**¼ fresh lemon**
2 medium-size egg yolks	**1 tablespoon fresh parsley**
¼ teaspoon Dijon mustard	**Salt and white pepper, to**
2 tablespoons honey	**taste**

Put sour cream into a small bowl. Beat egg yolks and mix well with the cream. Add mustard, honey, and the juice of ¼ fresh lemon. Stir thoroughly. Add parsley. Heat in a small skillet and serve hot, or allow to cool and serve chilled. Season to taste with salt and white pepper. *(Serves 4)*

Bluefish Normande

This recipe can be used for any full-flavored fish such as swordfish, red snapper, or mackerel. The sauce I like with it is a sweet cream sauce, made with hard apple cider (see next recipe).

2 1-pound fresh bluefish filets (one side of each filet should have skin intact)	1 tablespoon vegetable oil 1 tablespoon heavy cream ¼ cup bread crumbs

Preheat broiler. Wash and dry bluefish filets. Rub vegetable oil into the skin-covered side of the bluefish so it won't stick to the broiler surface. Turn fish over and rub half of the cream into the flesh of each filet. Sprinkle each filet evenly with bread crumbs, and place on broiler tray. Broil for 7 minutes or until fish flakes when tested with a fork. While fish broils, make the sauce. *(Serves 4)*

Sweet Cream Sauce

Be sure to use hard apple cider rather than sweet cider in this recipe; your local liquor store should have hard cider available.

1 small onion	1 teaspoon sweet basil
4 tablespoons sweet butter	2 tablespoons flour
½ cup hard apple cider	4 tablespoons milk
½ teaspoon fennel	1 cup heavy cream
1 bay leaf	Salt and white pepper

Peel onion and chop it into small pieces. Melt butter in a small skillet and sauté onion until it's transparent. Add cider, fennel, bay leaf, and sweet basil. Make a paste with the flour and milk. Add the heavy cream to the skillet, and bring to the boiling point. Thicken sauce with the flour and milk paste, stirring constantly to keep sauce smooth. After sauce thickens, reduce heat, and season to taste with salt and pepper. *(Serves 4)*

Garnish:

After you've made the sauce for the bluefish, and the fish has broiled for 7 minutes, open the broiler, and dot the fish with:

4 tablespoons butter

Sprinkle with:

Juice from ½ fresh lemon

Put fish back under broiler for a few seconds until the butter melts. Then put the fish onto a serving platter and serve the sauce in a separate container.

Soufflé Rothschild

This elegant dessert soufflé contains minced fruit and nuts; serve it with a chilled rum sauce (see recipe, below, and prepare before soufflé).

¼ cup minced candied fruit	2 cups milk
⅛ cup finely chopped nuts	½ teaspoon vanilla extract
5 tablespoons kirsch	3 egg yolks
½ cup flour	5 egg whites
¼ cup sugar	Confectioner's sugar

Preheat oven to 375° F. Butter a 9″ soufflé dish, and sprinkle it lightly and evenly with flour; set aside. Put fruit and nuts into a small bowl; add kirsch and set aside. Sift together flour and sugar; set aside. Put milk into a small saucepan, and bring just to boiling point; remove from heat, add vanilla, and stir. Pour half of the hot milk into the flour and sugar mixture; combine. Gradually add the mixture back into the remaining milk in the saucepan. Return saucepan to low heat, beating mixture with a whisk until it thickens. Remove from heat and set aside. Beat egg yolks and slowly whisk yolks into the milk mixture in the saucepan. Add fruit, nuts, and kirsch; stir and set aside. Beat egg whites into stiff peaks, and then thoroughly mix ⅓ of the whites into the soufflé mixture in the saucepan. Finally, gently fold in the remaining stiff egg whites and gently pour the soufflé into the soufflé dish. Bake for 25 minutes, then lightly dust the top with confectioner's sugar. Bake several minutes until sugar has melted; top of soufflé will look light golden brown. *(Serves 6)*

Rum Sauce

Make this sauce before you make the soufflé, so that it has time to chill. This sauce is also good served with fresh berries.

1 cup milk	½ teaspoon vanilla
4 egg yolks	4 tablespoons rum or ½
¼ cup sugar	teaspoon rum extract
Dash salt	2 tablespoons sugar
1 cup heavy cream	

Heat milk slowly in the top of a double boiler. Beat egg yolks in a small bowl and, using a whisk, add beaten egg yolks and ¼ cup of sugar to the milk. Continue whisking until mixture thickens. Add salt and remove from heat. In a medium-size bowl suitable for serving, combine heavy cream, vanilla, rum or rum extract, and sugar. Beat cream mixture until it stands in soft peaks. Gradually add the thickened custard in the saucepan to the whipped cream, stirring gently. Chill and serve with soufflé. *(Serves 6)*

Cheesecake

This is a very versatile cake. You may garnish it with your favorite fruit or with confectioner's sugar and cinnamon. You may also either beat the cream cheese until it's very smooth, or leave it less smooth for a chunkier texture. If you wish, some fruits may be added right into the batter; I like fresh pineapple. However you serve this cheesecake, the recipe makes one of the best I've ever tasted.

32 ounces cream cheese	1½ cups sugar
6 eggs	1½ cups heavy cream
2 tablespoons vanilla extract	½ cup sour cream
2 tablespoons flour	Juice from 1 fresh lemon

Preheat oven to 350° F. Soften cream cheese at room temperature. Beat eggs well, and add vanilla to the eggs. Combine flour and sugar; combine heavy cream and sour cream. In a very large bowl, alternately add sugar and flour mixture and cream mixture to cream cheese. Mix thoroughly until all the cream cheese is combined with all of the flour and sugar mixture and the creams. Add lemon juice and gently pour batter into a large spring form pan. Bake for 65 minutes, and then turn off oven, and leave cake in the oven for 30 minutes. Remove cake from the oven and allow to cool (it will settle slightly), and then refrigerate for 24 hours before slicing. *(Serves 10–12)*

Coffee Chocolate Mousse

Adding coffee to this chocolate mousse makes it very flavorful. Be sure to chill the mousse for at least 6 to 8 hours; it becomes firmer as it chills.

½ pound semi-sweet chocolate
½ cup strong black coffee
1 tablespoon honey
1 cup heavy cream
6 eggs

½ cup sugar
2 tablespoons cognac
½ teaspoon vanilla or almond
    extract
Dash salt

Melt chocolate in the top of a double boiler; add coffee, stir, and set aside. Combine honey with cream; whip until stiff and set aside. Separate egg whites from egg yolks, and beat the whites until very stiff; set aside. Beat egg yolks in a separate bowl. Gradually beat sugar, cognac, vanilla or almond extract, and dash of salt into the egg yolks. Add chocolate-coffee mixture to the yolks and mix well. Gradually fold whipped cream into the mixture, and then fold in the very stiff egg whites. Fold only until mousse is blended; you want to keep this dish light and airy. Chill for 6–8 hours before serving; you may chill overnight. *(Serves 6–8)*

Almond Fudge Cake

This is a very rich, thick batter, which makes a cake that's a cross between fudge and brownies. It is good topped with whipped cream and fruit, or ice cream.

4 eggs	1¾ cups sugar
4 squares semi-sweet baker's chocolate	½ cup flour
	½ cup ground almonds
½ pound sweet butter	⅛ teaspoon almond extract

Preheat oven to 350° F. Butter and flour a large 11″ ovenproof glass pie plate; set aside. Beat eggs and set them aside. Melt chocolate and sweet butter together over very low heat in the top of a double boiler. Gradually add sugar, flour, almonds, and extract; stir well. Add eggs last and pour batter into pie plate. Bake for 40 to 45 minutes or until a toothpick inserted in the center comes out clean. Be careful not to overbake; this batter is very thick and you want the center of the cake to remain moist. Cool cake and garnish as directed below. *(Serves 10–12)*

Topping for Almond Fudge Cake

1–2 cups heavy cream	1 teaspoon sugar
1 cup fresh raspberries or strawberries	1 teaspoon almond liqueur (optional)

Whip heavy cream and set it aside. Combine raspberries or strawberries with sugar and optional almond liqueur. Spread cream on top of the cake, and arrange fruit on top of the cream.

Fruit Pie

This is really a three-part recipe; the fruit pie consists of custard in a flaky crust covered with your choice of fruit and, if you wish, a fruit glaze for a bonus. *(Serves 6)*

Crust:

1 cup flour	½ cup softened sweet butter
½ teaspoon salt	1½ tablespoons water

Preheat oven to 350° F. Put flour into a large bowl and add salt. Crumble butter into flour, using your fingers or a pastry cutter. Gradually add water and continue mixing dough until a smooth, pliable dough forms. Roll out on a lightly floured board and fit into a 9″ pie pan. Bake for 10–12 minutes, until light brown. Remove from oven and cool. *(Makes one crust)*

Custard:

3 egg yolks	1¼ cups light cream
½ cup sugar	1 tablespoon melted butter
¼ cup cornstarch	½ teaspoon vanilla extract

Cream together egg yolks and sugar and set aside. In small saucepan, whisk cornstarch into cream. Continue whisking and add egg mixture. Slowly bring mixture to a boil over a low heat, whisking constantly so that custard is smooth and doesn't stick to the bottom of the pan. Continue whisking until custard begins to thicken. Stir in butter and whisk until custard is quite thick. Remove from heat and add vanilla. Stir and allow to cool slightly; our into baked pie crust and allow to cool completely. (This custard is also delicious served alone.)

Fruit:

Choose your favorite fruit. I find that any berry works very well (blueberries, strawberries, raspberries) or peaches, plums, or the exotic kiwi fruit. Wash and dry the fruit. If using peaches, plums, or kiwis, peel and slice them. Use ripe fresh fruits, about 2 cups. Sprinkle a little sugar on the fruit if you like a very sweet pie. Layer the fruit on top of the custard. Cover with whipped cream or the following glaze.

Fruit Glaze

1 cup fresh fruit   ¼ cup sugar
¼ cup water   Squeeze of fresh lemon juice

Use the same fruit that you choose for the pie. Crush the fruit, and combine it with water and sugar in a small saucepan. Heat and stir until sauce thickens. Add a squeeze of fresh lemon juice. Remove glaze from heat and cool until it's of a proper consistency to spread evenly over the top of the custard and fruit of the pie.

Baked Pears

Garnish these pears with whipped cream and the sauce in which they were baked.

4 ripe pears (Bosc are very good)	½ teaspoon cinnamon
1 cup dry red wine	½ cup sugar or honey
1 tablespoon lemon juice	2 tablespoons melted butter

Preheat oven to 350° F. Remove stems from pears; wash well and dry. Stand pears upright in a casserole dish. Combine remaining ingredients; pour liquid over pears and bake for 25–30 minutes. Chill before serving. *(Serves 4)*

Marinated Oranges

After a lavish meal, marinated oranges are a refreshing and welcome dessert. These may be made a day ahead of time and served after your dinner with crisp chocolate cookies (see following recipe).

2 cups water
1 cup sugar
5 navel oranges

2–3 tablespoons orange-flavored
liqueur

Combine in a saucepan the water, sugar, and the juice from one of the navel oranges. Bring liquid to a boil, reduce heat, and simmer 15 minutes. While liquid is simmering, peel remaining four oranges, and place side by side in a large bowl. (Peel away all of the skin and the underlying white membrane, so that you expose as much of the fruit as possible.) When the liquid has simmered for 15 minutes and has thickened into a light syrup, add 2–3 tablespoons of orange liqueur. Simmer another few minutes, then remove syrup from heat. Slowly add syrup to oranges, allow to cool, cover, and refrigerate. Allow to marinate overnight. *(Serves 4)*

Chocolate Crisps

These are the cookies that go well with marinated oranges. As each batch comes out of the oven, let the cookies cool slightly before taking them from the cookie sheet and placing them onto a cooling rack. These thin, wafer-like cookies are very rich. They're also excellent when served alone with coffee or milk.

½ cup melted sweet butter	1 egg
2 squares semi-sweet baker's chocolate	¾ cup flour
	¼ teaspoon salt
¾ cup brown sugar	½ teaspoon vanilla extract
¼ cup granulated sugar	

Preheat oven to 350° F. Melt butter and chocolate together over a very low flame. While butter melts, combine sugars and egg together in a large mixing bowl. Add melted butter-chocolate combination and stir to blend. Gradually add flour, mixing well to form a smooth batter. Add salt and vanilla and stir once more. Lightly butter a large cookie sheet, and drop batter onto the sheet using the teaspoon from a set of measuring spoons. (The amount of batter used should be a generous teaspoon, not leveled off.) Bake for 10–12 minutes. *(Makes about 36 cookies)*

Apple/Orange Marmalade

This is a treat at breakfast or any time.

2 pounds tart green cooking apples	1 navel orange
2 cups sugar	1 fresh lemon
1 cup water	Dash of salt

Peel, core, and slice apples. Put apples, sugar, and water into a large saucepan over low heat. Peel the orange and lemon; crush the fruit and add fruit juice and shredded fruit pulp to the apples. Chop orange and lemon peel into very small pieces; set aside. Simmer fruit for one hour, then add orange and lemon peel. Simmer additional 30 minutes. Put into jars according to when the marmalade will be used—see instructions under apple butter recipe, which follows. *(Makes 4–5 cups)*

Apple Butter

One of the many good things you can do with this apple butter is use it to make apple butter cookies; that recipe follows this one.

2 pounds tart green cooking apples	1 small piece of cheesecloth
1 large lemon	2–2½ cups sugar
1 cup water	Dash of salt
1 teaspoon pickling spices	¼ teaspoon cinnamon
	Dash of cloves

Peel, core, and thinly slice apples. Slice lemon and remove any seeds; do not peel. Put apples, lemon, and water into a large saucepan. Tie pickling spices in the cheesecloth, and add to the fruit. Bring to a boil, reduce heat, and simmer covered for 30 minutes or until the apples are tender. Remove pickling spices, cool fruit, and then purée in blender or food processor. Return puréed fruit to the saucepan, and bring to a boil. Add sugar, salt, cinnamon, and cloves. Reduce heat and simmer uncovered until mixture is very thick—about 2 hours. Stir frequently during simmering process, and remove foam that comes to the top.

If preparing for immediate serving, pour directly into sterilized jelly jars or large container. (Sterilize jars by submerging them in hot water; simmer jars for 15 minutes.) Cover and refrigerate. For long-term preservation, store in sterilized jelly glasses to within ½ inch from the top. Seal with ⅛ inch to ¼ inch of melted paraffin. Allow wax to cool and harden, cover glasses, and store in dry, cool, dark place. *(Makes 4 cups)*

Apple Butter Cookies

¼ cup sugar
½ cup melted butter
1 cup apple butter
2 cups flour
1 teaspoon baking soda
½ teaspoon baking powder

⅛ teaspoon salt
¼ cup milk
1 beaten egg
½ teaspoon vanilla extract
1 cup chopped nuts (walnuts or
pecans are good)

Preheat oven to 375° F. Combine sugar, melted butter, and apple butter in a large bowl. Sift together flour, baking soda, baking powder, and salt. Gradually add to bowl, stirring well. Add milk and beaten egg to mixture; stir well. Add vanilla and chopped nuts. Drop by teaspoon onto an ungreased cookie sheet. Bake for 8–10 minutes; cookies will puff up as they bake so leave room between each one. Cool and ice with the following icing. *(Makes about 48 cookies)*

Lemon Icing

⅔ cups confectioner's sugar
1½–2 tablespoons milk

Squeeze of fresh lemon
juice, about ¼ teaspoon

Combine the above in a small bowl. The icing will be thin; turn each cookie upside down and dip the top into the icing.

Walnut Pie

This dessert can be made ahead of time and then heated slightly just before serving. Top with whipped cream. For the best flavor try to use very fresh walnuts.

Crust:

1 cup flour	1 egg
½ cup sweet butter, softened at room temperature	Pinch of salt

Combine flour with butter, using your fingers or a pastry cutter to crumble together. Add egg and salt. (If the egg is rather small and the dough isn't moist enough, add a bit of milk.) Crumble together until a smooth dough is formed. Make a ball of dough, roll out on well-floured board, and place in a 9″ pie shell.

Filling:

1 cup light corn syrup	⅓ cup melted sweet butter
1 cup dark brown sugar	1 teaspoon vanilla extract
⅓ cup sour cream	3 eggs
Dash of salt	1½ cups whole shelled walnuts

Preheat oven to 350° F. Combine corn syrup, brown sugar, sour cream, salt, butter, and vanilla in a large bowl. Mix well. Beat eggs and add to the large bowl. Stir thoroughly and pour into uncooked pie crust. Sprinkle walnuts over the filling and bake for 45 minutes, or until filling is completely cooked. *(Serves 6)*

Carrot Cake

This is one of my favorite desserts.

3 cups sifted flour
2 teaspoons baking powder
2 teaspoons baking soda
3 teaspoons cinnamon
½ teaspoon salt
2 cups sugar
1¼ cups corn oil
2 teaspoons vanilla extract
4 large eggs

4 large grated raw carrots
   (about two generous cups)
1½ cups yellow raisins
1 cup chopped walnuts
1 cup drained crushed
   pineapple (optional)
Confectioner's sugar
   (optional)

Preheat oven to 350° F. Butter and flour two loaf pans; set aside. In a large mixing bowl, combine sifted flour, baking powder, baking soda, cinnamon, and salt. Add sugar. Gradually add corn oil, mixing well. Add vanilla and eggs, mix well, and add grated carrots. Add raisins and walnuts. If you like, add crushed pineapple. Stir well. The batter will be very, very thick and heavy. This yields a rich, moist cake that doesn't even need an icing. Bake for 55–60 minutes, or until a toothpick inserted into the center of the cake comes out clean. Be careful not to overbake; the cake should be very moist. After it has cooled, you may sprinkle the top of the cake with confectioner's sugar. *(Makes 2 loaf cakes)*

Thai Cuisine

Introduction

Siam, the country that provides the lush and exotic setting for Rodgers and Hammerstein's *The King And I*, was officially renamed Thailand in the late 1930s. The literal translation of "Thailand" is "land of the free," a very appropriate name since Thailand is the only southeast Asian country that never has been colonized by an outside power. Foreign interest in this small nation, which is roughly the same size as the state of Texas, has always been strong. In the late eighteenth and early nineteenth centuries, an influx of Chinese immigrants who became merchants and business entrepreneurs resulted in a rapid expansion of trade between the two countries. China, of course, wasn't the only nation interested in commerce. The British were trading with the Chinese Empire, and that whetted the British appetite for expanded Asian contacts. Siam politely received Western traders and signed limited treaties with the United Kindom and the United States. But these limited treaties led to greater Western demands for free trade and diplomatic representation. In Siam, these pressures were expertly met by King Mongkut—the monarch I portray on stage. Mongkut reigned from 1851 to 1868, and he was unusually adroit in his handling of foreign affairs. He also hired a British woman, Anna Leonowens, to teach in Siam, and theater audiences continue to applaud him for that.

One of Anna's pupils was King Mongkut's son and heir, Prince Chulalongkorn. When Chulalongkorn became king, he continued his father's policy of accommodation to the West. He also was a gourmet who had more than thirty wives. Each wife had her own cooks and her own kitchen. Pleasing the king was still a matter of great importance, and Chulalongkorn's wives often entered into friendly cooking competitions. To this day, many of the finest Thai gourmet chefs are women, and everyone treats them with utmost respect.

Thailand's climate is hot and humid, and it's easy to imagine your appetite waning as a result of the weather. The Thais, however, have the perfect stimulant for an appetite that needs a bit of prodding. They serve curries liberally spiced with hot chilies, and that really wakes up the taste buds. While to Western taste a curry may mean simply a hot, spicy food, Thai palates are very sophisticated and can distinguish many subtle flavors within a single curry. Although a chef in Bangkok can go to the market and buy a premixed curry paste, she usually prefers to grind her own at home with a mortar and pestle. A few of the spices and seasonings she'll choose from include coriander, cumin, peppercorns, tumeric, cinnamon, cardamom, cloves, nutmeg, garlic, and ginger. To enhance the curry, she uses red or green chili peppers. Please treat any chili peppers with respect, and treat chili peppers from Thailand with particular respect and even caution. They're very hot (especially the small ones) and you should use them sparingly until you become Thai in spirit and are accustomed to the peppers' piquant flavor. It may be wise to remove some of the seeds from the peppers you use in the following recipes. Grind them separately and, as you cook each curry, sample it and add the ground seeds to the sauce as your taste dictates. Since the seeds are the hottest part of the chilies, following this procedure will give you more control over the spiciness of the dish.

Besides individually ground chili pastes, Thai curries are distinguished by the addition of coconut cream, a liquid made from soaking fresh coconut meat in hot water. Coconut cream is a major ingredient used in Thai cooking and it's easy to make, as you'll see in the recipe section. The cream, which thickens during cooking, gives curries a smooth, rich texture. It's a versatile liquid that's also sometimes used in soups, salad dressings, and desserts.

You'll notice that the following recipes don't call for salt. Instead of mere salt, Thai cuisine substitutes "nam pla," a fish sauce which contains salt. Nam pla and lemon grass, another common seasoning used in this style of cooking, can be obtained by mail order or from specialty stores.

Because of the hot and humid climate, Thailand benefits from several rice harvests a year. As in other south Asian cuisines, rice plays a starring role surrounded by supporting side dishes. A typical meal usually includes soup, several curries, salad, and a meat or vegetable that's been cooked with very little sauce. (Foods are divided into "kaeng" or liquid dishes and "krueng kieng" or dry dishes. Kaeng refers to both curries and soups.) Noodles are also part of the Thai diet; the crispy rice vermicelli dish, for which we provide the recipe, can be served as an appetizer or as part of the main meal. Soup is considered a beverage and the soup pot is usually brought right to the table, where it sits on a little burner to stay warm. Salads are in keeping with the general spicy theme and are sprinkled with hot chilies.

What we call desserts, which are usually reserved for the finishing touches, are available throughout the day in Thailand as between-meal snacks. At the markets, vendors sell sweets wrapped in coconut leaves. For a dish which follows a meal and serves as dessert, Thais prefer fresh fruits and, on occasion, custard. The tropical fruits they traditionally serve include guavas, mangoes, litchis, papayas, pomelos, bananas, pineapples, and coconuts.

Serve tea, fruit juice, coffee lightened with condensed or evaporated milk, or fresh ice water flavored subtly with rose petals with your Thai meal. With the help of the following recipes you'll be able to treat all your guests royally.

Substitutions and Equivalents

Nam Pla

Nam pla is a fish sauce made with anchovies; it is used instead of salt in Thai cooking. You can order nam pla from mail-order outlets or you can use the following recipe for a sauce that tastes similar to nam pla. Simply add as much as you like to accent the flavor of each dish calling for nam pla. This sauce is always added according to individual taste.

1 teaspoon anchovy paste
4 teaspoons soy sauce

4 teaspoons water

Combine all of the above and mix well. This usually yields enough sauce to adequately season several dishes. Refrigerate any leftover sauce in a tightly covered container.

Palm Sugar

Palm sugar resembles walnut fudge in appearance and flavor. You can substitute brown sugar for palm sugar.

Chilies

Order hot dried chilies from mail-order stores if none can be had at local gourmet or specialty food shops. If you can't obtain Thai chilies, try flaked cayenne instead. Spice stores usually carry fresh flaked cayenne, which is hotter than pepper that has been stored for a while. You can also use the small, hot red and green chili peppers available in most supermarkets or vegetable stores.

Curry

All Thai curries are combinations of various spices and seasonings. In Thailand, all these spices can be purchased and ground fresh daily. The recipes we've chosen contain seasonings readily available outside Thailand, such as coriander, cinnamon, cumin, tumeric, and garlic.

Garnishes

Thai cuisine produces colorful and lovely dishes. Serve the main courses on platters or in shallow bowls, and garnish as you wish from your choice of the following:

Shredded red and green fresh
  chilies (remove seeds if
  desired)
Coriander leaves
Slices of fresh lime
Pineapple wedges

Maraschino cherries
Shredded scallion
Fresh cucumber wedges or
  thick slices with serrated
  edges

Tod Mun Pla

These are fried fish balls, one of the most traditional of Thai appetizers. Serve them with the following recipe for cucumber sauce.

1½ pounds cod filets	1 slice fresh ginger, minced
3 cloves garlic	3 dried small hot chili peppers
12 black peppercorns	(or flaked cayenne to taste)
2 tablespoons fresh parsley	2 tablespoons soy sauce
½ teaspoon cilantro (coriander)	Vegetable oil in deep fat fryer

Make sure all bones are removed from the fish. Grind the fish together with all of the seasonings and the soy sauce. Shape into balls about 1″ in diameter, and fry in hot vegetable oil until the fish balls are brown and crispy, about 4 minutes. *(Serves 6)*

Cucumber Sauce

2 large cucumbers	⅛ cup light corn syrup
1 small onion	Nam pla to taste
½ cup vinegar	¼ cup crushed roasted unsalted
½ teaspoon lemon grass°	peanuts

Peel and slice cucumbers. Peel and slice onion very thin. Combine vinegar, lemon grass, and corn syrup; season to taste with nam pla. Pour dressing over cucumbers and marinate several hours. Before serving, sprinkle with crushed peanuts. *(Serves 6)*

°Lemon grass can be purchased in a dried, stalklike form that must be soaked in water before use. There is also powdered lemon grass, which you may add according to individual taste.

Thai Salad

The typical Thai salad combines vegetables, fruit and, in this recipe, shrimp.

2 cups shredded cabbage	5 tablespoons peanut oil
1 cup cooked shrimp	2 egg yolks
¼ cup chopped green pepper	Nam pla to taste
1 papaya	Crushed red chili pepper to
1 fresh lemon or lime	taste

Combine cabbage, shrimp, and green pepper in a large bowl. Peel and remove seeds from the papaya; cut into bite-size pieces and squeeze the juice of half the fresh lemon or lime over the papaya; add to salad. Combine juice from the second half of the lemon or lime with the peanut oil. Beat the egg yolks and add to the fruit juice and oil. Stir well, add nam pla to taste, and add dressing to salad. Toss well, sprinkle with red chili peppers to taste, and serve. *(Serves 4)*

Clear Shrimp Soup

This soup is spicy, although in Thailand it would be considered rather mild. Don't be afraid to reduce the amount of chilies—cook according to taste.

8 cups chicken stock
½ teaspoon powdered lemon grass
¼ teaspoon crushed red chili pepper
Nam pla to taste
½ pound fresh shrimp

1 cup sliced fresh mushrooms
3 tablespoons fresh lime juice
3 shredded hot green chili peppers
4–6 small fresh coriander leaves
2 chopped scallions

Bring stock to boil in a large saucepan. Add lemon grass, red chili, and nam pla. Simmer 15 minutes. While soup simmers, peel, clean, and devein shrimp. Add shrimp and simmer 10 minutes. Add mushrooms, simmer 2 minutes. Stir in lime juice and green chili peppers. Simmer additional 2 minutes. Garnish with coriander and scallion. *(Serves 6)*

Hot and Sour Soup

Thai soups are designed to make you feel warm and cozy inside. This one combines sweet and sour flavors.

6 cups chicken stock	1 teaspoon brown sugar
2 large chicken breasts, cooked	1 tablespoon soy sauce
2 tablespoons lemon juice	¼ teaspoon crushed or flaked
1 cup roast pork, cooked	red chili pepper (more or
1 large fresh tomato	less to taste)

Bring stock to boil in a large saucepan. While soup is coming to a boil, shred the chicken meat. When soup reaches boil, add chicken and lemon juice, and reduce heat. Cut pork into thin strips; add to soup. Slice tomato and cut each slice into quarters. Add tomato, sugar, soy, and chili peppers. Simmer for several minutes and then serve. *(Serves 6)*

Sautéed Mixed Vegetables

This side dish is a delight to behold—it's like the bounty of a vegetable garden on your dining table.

1 cup shredded white cabbage	1 tablespoon palm or brown
1 green pepper	sugar
1 medium onion	2 tablespoons water
1 small bunch fresh broccoli	1 tablespoon soy sauce
2 cups fresh pea sprouts	4 dried hot red chili peppers (or
6 tablespoons vegetable oil	flaked cayenne to taste)
3 garlic cloves	

Blanch shredded cabbage by placing it into boiling water for one minute. Remove cabbage from water, rinse in cool water and drain; set aside. Devein and remove seeds from green pepper; cut into thin strips. Peel onion and slice thinly; separate slices into rings. Cut broccoli into small spears about 3″ long, and discard bottom parts of stalk. Wash and drain sprouts. Heat oil in a wok or large skillet. Crush garlic and sauté in hot oil. Add, in order, onion, broccoli, green pepper, and cabbage. Sauté each vegetable for 2 minutes before adding the next vegetable. After adding the cabbage, mix together sugar, water, soy, and red chili pepper. Pour over vegetables, stir, add sprouts, cook one minute, and serve. *(Serves 4-6)*

Thai Crispy Noodles with Sweet Sauce (Mee Krob)

This dish is intriguing. The noodles cook in several seconds; when you put them into hot oil they sink to the bottom of the fryer and almost instantly rise to the top. Remove them from the oil as soon as they come up; if you leave them to fry any longer they'll be overdone. Cook the noodles in small batches so that the oil stays hot. The sauce that coats the noodles is like a light syrup; the noodles are crunchy and yet tender and their taste is out of this world.

2 eggs	2 tablespoons palm or brown
1 tablespoon vegetable oil	sugar
4 scallions	2 shredded red chili peppers
Vegetable oil in a deep fryer	Nam pla to taste
6 ounces rice noodles	½ cup cooked shrimp, in small
(vermicelli)	pieces
2 tablespoons vegetable oil	½ cup cooked pork, in small
2 garlic cloves, minced	pieces
2 tablespoons water	Lettuce (optional)

Lightly beat eggs. Heat 1 tablespoon vegetable oil in a large skillet and cook eggs in a thin omelette. Remove omelette from pan, cool and shred; set shredded egg aside. Cut scallion into 2″ pieces; set aside. Heat vegetable oil in a deep-fat fryer. While the oil heats, break the vermicelli into small rectangular sections. To test the oil for the correct heat, drop one strand of noodle into the oil. If the strand puffs up and immediately comes to the surface, the oil is ready. Cook the vermicelli a bit at a time, removing them from the fryer as soon as they rise to the top of the oil, and set the cooked noodles aside on paper towels to drain. Heat 2 tablespoons vegetable oil in a wok or large skillet. Sauté minced garlic in hot oil. Combine water, palm sugar, chili peppers, and nam pla and add the combination to the pan. Stir several minutes until a light syrup forms. Add shrimp and pork; stir to coat with syrup. Add cooked noodles, turning so that noodles are also coated with the syrup mixture. Transfer noodles to a heated serving dish and garnish with shredded egg and scallion. If you like, you may serve mee krob on a bed of lettuce. *(Serves 4)*

Soft Boon Noodles

The texture of these noodles is completely opposite from that of the crispy noodles; they're very soft and they're absolutely clear after they're cooked.

6 ounces clear rice noodles (vermicelli)	3 teaspoons palm or brown sugar
2 tablespoons vegetable oil	2 tablespoons water
2 cloves minced garlic	Nam pla to taste
16 small shrimp, cleaned and deveined	2 eggs
	3 small green chilies, chopped
	2 scallions, chopped

Cook vermicelli in a saucepan of boiling water for several minutes; the noodles will be clear and they should have a slightly al dente texture. Do not overcook; they'll be done after only several minutes in the water. Drain noodles and set them aside. Heat oil in a large skillet. Sauté minced garlic in oil, and then add shrimp, cooking for several minutes until the shrimp turn pink. Combine sugar, water, and nam pla. Add to the pan. Beat eggs and add to the pan. Before the eggs cook, add the noodles and stir until the eggs are cooked. Remove the noodles to a serving platter, and garnish with chopped green chilies and chopped scallions. *(Serves 4)*

Coconut Cream

Coconut cream is an indispensible ingredient in the preparation of some Thai curries. Besides giving the dish a subtle, sweet flavor, the coconut cream acts as a natural thickener for sauces. Unsweetened natural coconut cream is available for purchase from mail-order suppliers. It's easy to make your own, however, from fresh coconuts purchased in your local markets.

Shake the coconut to make sure there is liquid inside; the more liquid the coconut contains, the more likely it is to be fresh. Puncture the "eyes" of the coconut and drain the liquid; this coconut milk is discarded or drunk. Crack open the coconut and remove the meat from the shell. Use a sharp knife to scrape the thin brown skin from the white coconut meat. Grate the coconut meat by hand or with a food processor. Measure the amount of grated coconut, and set the coconut aside. Measure into a saucepan a volume of water or milk equal to the volume of coconut meat. Heat the liquid to boiling, and pour it over the grated coconut. Soak coconut meat for 30 minutes, and then strain the resulting liquid through a cheesecloth. Discard the pulp.

Store in the refrigerator, and use within a day or two. The coconut cream has a natural tendency to separate; just stir it before using. Coconut cream may also be frozen for future use. *(Each cup of coconut meat soaked in liquid will yield about a cup of strained coconut cream.)*

Sautéed Chicken with Hot Curry

This curry has a spicy aftertaste that is tempered by the coconut cream.

2 pounds chicken pieces	½ teaspoon coriander
4 tablespoons vegetable oil	1 teaspoon cumin
4 scallions	2 cups chicken stock
2 cloves garlic	½ cup coconut cream
1 teaspoon lemon grass	6–8 dried hot red chili peppers
¼ teaspoon black pepper	

Remove skin from chicken and cut into pieces about 3″ x 2″. Wash and dry chicken pieces. Cut scallion into 2″ lengths, and crush garlic. Soak the lemon grass in a small amount of water for a few minutes, then mince the softened stalk. Heat vegetable oil in a Dutch oven. Sauté scallion and garlic in hot oil for several minutes. Add chicken and brown it on both sides. Reduce heat and combine lemon grass, pepper, coriander, and cumin. Mix spices with chicken stock and coconut cream; pour over chicken. Cook covered for one hour. Remove cover, add chili peppers, and cook uncovered for 30 more minutes. *(Serves 4)*

Chicken with Yellow Curry

This curry is very mild and has a sweet taste because it is cooked with cinnamon.

3 cups coconut cream
1 large onion, sliced
1 large bay leaf
2 pounds chicken in pieces,
    with bone and skin
    removed

½ teaspoon tumeric
½ teaspoon cinnamon
1 teaspoon coriander
4 dried hot red chili peppers
1 clove garlic
½ fresh lime

Heat two of the cups of coconut cream in a large saucepan. When liquid reaches boiling point, reduce heat, and add onion and bay leaf. Stir and add chicken pieces. Simmer slowly for one hour. After one hour, combine tumeric, cinnamon, and coriander. Add to the chicken and stir well. Add chili peppers and garlic. Add reserved cup of coconut cream to thin the sauce. Simmer 10–15 minutes, and, just before serving, sprinkle with the juice of half a fresh lime. *(Serves 4)*

Beef with Basil

This dish has a most amazing taste, a combination of sweet and slightly spicy flavors, that is unequalled in any other style of cooking. The sauce should boil for the last few minutes of cooking, so that it caramelizes and coats the meat.

2 pounds of sirloin
4 tablespoons vegetable oil
2 cloves garlic
4 tablespoons palm or brown
   sugar

2 tablespoons water
  Nam pla to taste
2 sliced fresh hot red chilies
4 tablespoons fresh basil leaves,
   or ½ tablespoon dried basil

Cut sirloin into bite-size cubes; set aside. Heat vegetable oil in a heavy skillet. Sauté garlic in oil. While garlic cooks, combine sugar and water; set aside. Add meat to skillet, cooking on all sides. When meat is almost done, add sugar and water. Simmer slowly until meat is cooked through, add sliced chilies, and increase heat. Allow sauce to caramelize and coat the meat; this will take only a minute or two. Add basil, stir, and serve at once. *(Serves 4)*

Beef Masaman Curry

If, while the beef cooks, you mix together the spices that make the curry, you can add the spices to the meat a little bit at a time. This way, you can completely control the strength of the curry. This flavor is hearty and refreshing because of the lime juice added at the very end.

2½ pounds stew beef, in chunks	1 teaspoon cardamom
2 garlic cloves	½ teaspoon cloves
1 large onion, sliced	½ teaspoon nutmeg
3 cups coconut cream	½ teaspoon cinnamon
6–8 small dried hot red chilies	1 teaspoon sugar
10 black peppercorns	1 fresh lime
1 teaspoon coriander	¾ cup roasted unsalted peanuts

Trim excess fat from beef chunks; set aside. In a large Dutch oven, combine garlic cloves, sliced onion, and coconut cream. Add beef and simmer covered over a low heat for 1½ hours. Add chilies and peppercorns. Combine coriander, cardamom, cloves, nutmeg, and cinnamon. After beef has cooked for 1½ hours, gradually add the spice mix to the sauce, tasting as you go until it's as strong as you like. Add the sugar and simmer for another ½ hour with the cover off. Remove from heat and add the juice of one fresh lime. Place onto a heated platter, and sprinkle roasted unsalted peanuts over the curry just before serving. *(Serves 6)*

Thai Dipping Sauce (Nam Prik)

In Thailand, this is one of the sauces set out on every table for use with any curry. It brings out the flavor of any food you dip into it.

½ cup nam pla*
½ cup fresh lime juice

8 hot dried red chilies
1 small onion, in thin slices

Combine nam pla, lime juice, and chilies, stir. Add onion slices. Allow to marinate for several hours. The sauce will become spicier as it marinates; adjust the amount of chilies according to taste. *(Makes about 1 cup)*

Spicy Shredded Pork

You may substitute beef or chicken for the pork in this dish.

2 pounds pork loin roast
4 tablespoons soy sauce
2 tablespoons fresh lime juice
1 teaspoon sugar
½ teaspoon minced fresh ginger
½ teaspoon coriander

4 small hot dried red chili
   peppers
4 tablespoons vegetable oil
1 garlic clove, peeled and
   crushed

Shred pork; set aside. Combine soy sauce, lime juice, sugar, minced ginger, coriander, and red chili. Place pork into a large bowl and pour sauce over meat. Allow to marinate one hour. Heat vegetable oil in a large skillet; saute garlic in hot oil. Add pork and marinade to skillet; cook until pork is well-done and most of the marinade has been absorbed into the meat. *(Serves 4)*

---

*See Substitutions and Equivalents, page 193.

Sweet and Sour Shrimp

This dish has the perfect combination of flavors—sweet, tart, a hint of spiciness—and a lovely array of colors because of the tomato and red and green peppers used in the sauce.

16 large shrimp
2–3 tablespoons flour
   Vegetable oil in a deep fryer
1 medium onion
¼ cup vegetable oil
2 garlic cloves
2 fresh green chili peppers, sliced

4 dried hot red chili peppers
2 medium-size ripe tomatoes, sliced and then cut into quarters
¼ cup chicken stock
2 tablespoons sugar
1 tablespoon vinegar
3 tablespoons soy sauce

Clean, peel, and devein shrimp; wash and dry well. Dust flour over the shrimp. Heat vegetable oil in a deep fryer and fry shrimp several minutes until they're light golden brown. Set aside to drain on paper towels. Peel and slice onion; cut slices in half. Heat ¼ cup vegetable oil in a large skillet. Sauté onion in oil until onion is transparent. Add garlic to pan, then green chilies, stir. Add red chili peppers and tomatoes. Reduce heat and mix stock with sugar, vinegar, and soy sauce. Add to pan and simmer several minutes. Arrange shrimp on heated serving platter, pour vegetables and sauce over shrimp, and serve. *(Serves 4)*

Thai Ginger Fish

Use a whole fish, with head and tail intact, or cod filets.

1 2-pound cod	2 tablespoons soy sauce
2 tablespoons cornstarch	2 tablespoons minced scallion
1 tablespoon flour	3 slices fresh ginger, cut in thin
¼ cup vegetable oil	strips
4 tablespoons vinegar	1 tablespoon cornstarch
4 tablespoons palm or brown	2 tablespoons water
sugar	4–6 hot dried red chili peppers
1 cup chicken stock	

Wash and dry fish. Combine cornstarch and flour, and coat both sides of fish with the mixture. Heat vegetable oil in a large skillet, and fry fish until it is golden brown on each side and flesh flakes easily with a fork. Place cooked fish on paper towels to drain, and then place fish on a heated serving platter. To prepare sauce, combine vinegar, sugar, stock, and soy sauce in a small saucepan. Heat to boiling point, reduce heat, and add scallion and ginger. Simmer one minute. Combine cornstarch and water; add to sauce and stir constantly until sauce thickens. Add chili peppers, simmer one more minute, and then pour sauce over fish. (*Serves 4*)

Creamed Bananas

Another way to make this dish is to use commercially prepared coconut cream available in most supermarkets—see note in recipe (this is the cream used to prepare piña coladas).

3 ripe bananas	4 tablespoons palm or brown
1 cup coconut cream	sugar
	¼ teaspoon vanilla extract

Peel bananas and slice into 1" pieces. Heat coconut cream in a small saucepan over a low flame. When cream is hot, add sugar, and stir until sugar dissolves. Add sliced bananas and vanilla, stir to coat, and serve warm. (Note: If using commercial coconut cream, simply heat it and add the bananas and vanilla to the heated cream.) *(Serves 4)*

Coconut Rice Custard

This is the Thai version of rice pudding.

2 cups coconut cream	8 eggs
1 cup brown sugar	1 cup cooked white rice

Preheat oven to 375° F. Combine coconut cream and brown sugar, or use 3 cups commercially prepared coconut cream (see above recipe). Put mixture into saucepan, and simmer until liquid reaches boiling point. Reduce heat so that mixture simmers. Beat eggs and add to mixture, once again bringing custard to the boiling point. Simmer and stir for at least 5 minutes, until custard thickens. Add cooked rice and continue to stir custard as it simmers for a few minutes to heat rice through.

Pour custard into a baking dish with a tight-fitting cover. Cover custard and place baking dish into a pan filled with hot water. Place pan with the baking dish into the oven, and steam for 30 minutes. Check to see if custard is ready by inserting a knife into the middle of the custard; if the knife comes out clean, the custard is done. If not, bake a few minutes longer. Serve warm or cold. *(Serves 6)*

Fresh Fruit with Iced Syrup

Use fruits such as mango, papaya, pineapple, melon, coconut, bananas, and palm nut (pomelo) for a true Thai dessert. Make the syrup first and then let it cool, so that it will thicken when you pour it over the ice.

1 cup water
½ cup sugar
1 teaspoon jasmine flavoring
   (optional)

4 cups sliced fresh fruit
2 cups crushed ice

Combine water, sugar, and jasmine flavoring in a small saucepan. Heat to boiling, reduce heat, and simmer 10 minutes. Remove pan from heat and set aside. Arrange four cups of fresh fruit of your choice in a serving bowl. Crush ice in a blender or food processor until it's the consistency of snow. Spread ice over top of fruit and pour syrup over ice. *(Serves 6)*

Mail-Order Suppliers

(You may wish to write and request catalogs before placing your order.)

Lekvar by the Barrel
(H. Roth & Son)
1577 First Avenue
New York, New York 10028

(212) 734-1110

Almost anything you need for any type of cuisine can be found here, including utensils and specialty items such as fish steamers.

Katagiri, Inc.
224 East 59th Street
New York, New York 10022

(212) 755-3566

Japanese

K. Tanaka Co., Inc., Grocers
326 Amsterdam Avenue
New York, New York 10023

(212) 874-6600

Japanese, some Chinese

Aphrodisia
282 Bleecker Street
New York, New York 10014

(212) 989-6440

Thai

Wing Fat
35 Mott Street
New York, New York 10013

(212) 962-0433

Chinese

There are numerous stores that do not mail their merchandise but are wondrous to explore when in any large city. If you're in New York, one of the best places to go for Thai ingredients is Poo Ping, at 81A Bayard Street, (212) 349-7662. This store is located in the city's Chinatown area, and you can wander from shop to shop and purchase enough to stock your kitchen generously.

Metric Measure Conversion Table
(Approximations)

When You Know (U.S.)	Multiply by	To Find (Metric)
	WEIGHT	
ounces	28	grams
pounds	0.45	kilograms
	VOLUME	
teaspoons	5	milliliters
tablespoons	15	milliliters
fluid ounces	30	milliliters
cups	0.24	liters
pints	0.47	liters
quarts	0.95	liters
	TEMPERATURE	
degrees Fahrenheit (°F)	subtract 32° and multiply the remainder by 5/9 or .556	degrees Celsius or Centigrade (°C)

Index

215